Collected Sonnets   ...d New

Charles Tennyson Turner

COLLECTED SONNETS

OLD AND NEW

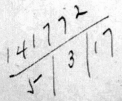

BY

CHARLES TENNYSON TURNER

LONDON
C. KEGAN PAUL & CO., 1 PATERNOSTER SQUARE
1880

TO

EDMUND LUSHINGTON

THIS VOLUME

IS AFFECTIONATELY INSCRIBED

TO

EDMUND LUSHINGTON

THIS VOLUME

IS AFFECTIONATELY INSCRIBED

MIDNIGHT, JUNE 30, 1879.

I.

Midnight—in no midsummer tune
  The breakers lash the shores :
The cuckoo of a joyless June
  Is calling out of doors :

And thou hast vanish'd from thine own
  To that which looks like rest,
True brother, only to be known
  By those who love thee best.

II.

Midnight—and joyless June gone by,
  And from the deluged park
The cuckoo of a worse July
  Is calling thro' the dark :

But thou art silent underground,
  And o'er thee streams the rain,
True poet, surely to be found
  When Truth is found again.

III.

And, now to these unsummer'd skies
 The summer bird is still,
Far off a phantom cuckoo cries
 From out a phantom hill ;

And thro' this midnight breaks the sun
 Of sixty years away,
The light of days when life begun,
 The days that seem to-day,

When all my griefs were shared with thee,
 And all my hopes were thine—
As all thou wert was one with me,
 May all thou art be mine !

A. TENNYSON.

CHARLES TENNYSON, born at Somersby, in the county of Lincoln, July 4, 1808, was the second son of the Reverend George Clayton Tennyson, LL.D., Rector of Somersby and Enderby, and vicar of Great Grimsby. The childhood of Charles was passed in Somersby; in later life he would often recall with affection his early haunts, the gray hill near the Rectory, the winding lanes shadowed by tall elm-trees, and the two brooks that meet at the bottom of the glebe-field. He was sent for some years of boy-hood to the grammar-school of Louth; afterwards his father undertook his education at home, until he became an undergraduate of Trinity College, Cambridge. While there he obtained a Bell scholarship, chiefly, I have heard, on account of the exquisite poetical English into which he translated the Greek and Roman classics. Among his friends he was held to be a rising poet. His college-contemporaries who still remain remember the fine face with the dark eyes and hair, and the look of Southern Europe about him that made Thackeray, seeing him in middle manhood, call him a 'Velasquez tout craché.'

Having graduated 1832, and been ordained 1835, he was appointed curate of Tealby, and eventually vicar of Grasby, a lonely village on the Lincolnshire Wolds. By the will of a relative, who bequeathed him a small estate, his surname of 'Tennyson' was exchanged for that of 'Turner.' In 1837 he married Louisa Sellwood. They took up their abode in their house at Caistor, three miles from Grasby ; then, that they might be among their parishioners, in the ruinous and deserted vicarage of Grasby itself. Illness compelled them both to quit this, and to be for a long while absent from Lincolnshire. When they returned to the parish, it was to live there nearly thirty years— he the bountiful and loving father of his flock, she in all things his devoted helpmate. At their own expense they built the new vicarage, the new church, and the schools. They seldom left home except during harvest-time for a holiday in Wales, Scotland, or elsewhere. Of late his health had been slowly failing ; and on April 25, 1879, he died peacefully at Cheltenham, whither he had gone to be under the care of his old friend Dr. Ker. His wife survived her husband less than a month.

A mere obituary sketch scarcely admits of detail, otherwise many anecdotes might be told of his delight in his garden, of his fondness for his dogs, of his training his horses to obey his voice rather than rein or whip, and of his playful gentleness with children. No one, however, who reads his poems, can well fail to perceive the 'alma beata e bella ' breathing through them ; and those who best knew him feel that in these he almost lives again as he was in his daily life. Yet, when I talked with him a year ago, nothing of what he had written seemed to me to represent in full measure that simplicity of the man—at once childlike and heroic.

The worth of his work has been shown by an abler hand than mine in a most kindly and comprehensive review, which, through the courtesy of the Editor of the 'Nineteenth Century,' we have been allowed to transfer to the following pages. I may add that in my Father's judgment some of the sonnets have all the tenderness of the Greek epigram, and that he ranks a few of them among the noblest in our language.

HALLAM TENNYSON.

1880

CONTENTS.

———◆———

SONNETS PUBLISHED IN 1864 AND DEDICATED TO ALFRED TENNYSON.

CONTENTS.   XV

a

CONTENTS.

SONNETS PUBLISHED IN 1873 AND DEDI-
CATED TO AGNES GRACE WELD.

xx CONTENTS.

SONNETS NOW FIRST PUBLISHED, EXCEPT FOUR OR FIVE, WHICH HAVE APPEARED IN MAGAZINES.

LYRICS.

INTRODUCTORY ESSAY.

In an obituary notice of the late Charles Turner—
Alfred Tennyson's elder brother—I find the following
description of his character as a poet. 'He had a
very considerable gift of tender fancy and of plaintive
elegiac melody, but he was lacking in a sense of style ;
his writings are chiefly sonnets, and they are mostly
very incorrect in form.'

As to his gift of fancy and melody, everybody who
has read any of his poems will agree. But in saying
that his sonnets are '*incorrect* in *form*'[1] the writer can
only have meant that the rhymes do not follow the
order prescribed either by the Miltonic or the Shakes-
pearian sonnet ; and in imputing to him a lack of
the 'sense of style' he must, I suppose, have meant
the same thing ; for otherwise it would be hard to say
what he can have meant. Now, as a sonnet is sup-
posed to be a thing complete in itself, to be read

---

[1] 'Among the 285 sonnets contained in the three volumes,
there are two which are really incorrect in form, each having
two rhymeless lines. But this has evidently been by oversight
—the result probably of careless correction. In the sonnet en-
titled 'The Higher Criticism,' p. 173, 'rise,' in the tenth line,
should plainly have been altered to 'mount.' In 'Little Nora,'
p. 277, the first line should have ended with 'drew' instead of
gave.'

B

without reference to what goes before or after, there can be no good reason for requiring all sonnets to be made on the same model.   Even the conventional limit as to length is purely artificial.   It can have no foundation in nature, and its only use in art is to supply a poet with something to do when his invention fails.   He can at any rate invent rhyming lines enough to complete a self-imposed task ; which in that unhappy case will seem to be something.   But though the poet is helped, I doubt whether poetry is ever the better for it.   If Horace had not allowed himself to write an ode in more or fewer than four stanzas, would his books of odes have presented finer specimens of the art?   The necessity of forcing the thought into the frame has spoiled many good sonnets,[1]

---

[1] Wordsworth in a winter's walk saw in a hedge a bird's nest filled with snow.   It struck him as an emblem of a warm heart forsaken, and suggested a sonnet.   A lover remonstrates with his mistress on her silence, and exclaims :—

'Speak! though this soft warm heart, once free to hold
A thousand tender pleasures, thine and mine,
Be left more desolate, more dreary cold,
Than a forsaken bird's nest filled with snow
'Mid its own bush of leafless eglantine—
Speak—that my torturing doubts their end may know.'

What more was wanted?   There were wanted eight opening lines ; the first, fourth, fifth, and seventh ending with one rhyme, and the second, third, sixth, and eighth, with another.   Correctness of form required them.   Of course they could be supplied ; and here they are :—

'Why art thou silent?   Is thy love a plant
Of such weak fibre that the treacherous air
Of absence withers what was once so fair?
Is there no debt to pay, no boon to grant?

and it would be hard to show how it can have improved any ; since whenever the poet found that what he had to say could be better expressed in fourteen lines than in more or fewer, the regular fourteen were always at his service.

Some virtue there may possibly be in this particular number (though it is hard to believe it) which accounts for so general an agreement among poets to endure the restraint. But to insist that, besides an artificial limit in length, there shall be in every sonnet the same artificial arrangement of rhymes, a departure from which shall be held to imply the want of a 'sense of style,' seems altogether unreasonable. For upon this point there has been no such general agreement. No man could write better sonnets in the Miltonic metre than Keats. But as his taste matured he lost his liking for it. He not only felt the rhymes to be unnecessary fetters, but their order to be ungraceful ; proposed to seek for a better—for

> Sandals more interwoven and complete
> To fit the naked foot of poesy—

and meanwhile in all his later sonnets used the Shakes-

> Yet have my thoughts for thee been vigilant
> (As would my deeds have been) with hourly care ;
> The mind's least generous wish a mendicant
> For nought but what thy happiness could spare.'

The *form* is now correct: but will anybody say that the poem is improved? The origin of this sonnet is historical. If we had an account of the composition, I think it would be found that the last six lines were composed first, and that the first eight were put in after, not because the expression of the thought, but only because the form of the sonnet, required them.

pearian form,—with an occasional variation to avoid
the monotony of the concluding couplet. But it is
needless to call witnesses. To say that the Miltonic
and the Shakespearian systems of rhyme are the *only*
forms in which a poetic thought can be adequately
expressed in fourteen lines is manifestly as extravagant
as it would be to deny that for the expression of *some*
poetic thoughts they are in their several ways the best
forms that have been tried. The Miltonic arrange-
ment makes a stately and imposing measure, admirably
fitted for the expression of certain exalted moods of
mental emotion, and for that very reason *not* so well
fitted for the expression of other moods. The Shakes-
pearian, on the contrary, is one of the simplest,
easiest, and most natural of measures ; requires no
education of the ear—no curious disposition of
rhyme ; and can express anything which our familiar
elegiac quatrain with alternate rhymes would be capa-
ble of expressing in three stanzas with help of a
rhyming couplet at the end. But both these arrange-
ments have the disadvantage—a disadvantage both to
writer and reader—of a want of freedom in modulation.
The Shakespearian admits of no variation in the order
of rhymes at all ; and though the Miltonic allows
liberty enough in the rhyming arrangement of the last
six lines, yet the artificial and peculiar movement of
the first eight so predominates in the general effect
that many sonnets of that structure can hardly be read
one after another without wish for a change. The
form of sonnet which Charles Turner chose for him-
self from the first—and I think invented, though per-
haps without knowing it—admits of much greater

variety than either of these ; leaves the metrical move-
ment free to follow the natural movement of the
thought, and finds room within its prison of fourteen
lines for modulations enough to relieve the reader
from all sense of monotony, and freedom enough to
give to the writer the full command (within the pre-
scribed limit) of the fittest metrical expression for
whatever he wants to express. How considerable the
variety is which he obtains by this liberty may be
judged from the fact that in the first thirty-four son-
nets of his earliest volume, though one arrangement is
four times repeated, and two others twice, I find
among the remaining twenty-six no two in which the
rhymes follow in exactly the same order. And yet
they always fall so naturally into their places, that I
doubt whether anyone not engaged in a critical
examination of the question would be conscious of
any differences in metrical structure, or be able to say
offhand where they are or what they consist in. In-
deed, I think it possible that the writer himself did
not know, and that the only rule he went by was to
arrange his rhymes in each case in the order which
seemed to give most of the effect that he wanted.

But however the metre of each sonnet may be
varied within its own limits, a volume of short poems
independent of each other will always be like a gallery
of pictures ; where each is seen to disadvantage, be-
cause the attention is disturbed and distracted by its
neighbours. Hawthorne says somewhere that, to take
in the meaning of a picture, you must be alone with
it. To appreciate a collection of sonnets, you should
read them one by one, with intervals between, long

enough to let the impression of each get out of the other's way. It is this which gives such collections a bad chance with professional critics, whose business it is to pronounce judgment without delay upon all volumes that are brought before them ; and this is probably the true excuse and explanation of the negligence of our purveyors of literary intelligence in distinguishing and making known the rare and exquisite and original genius which lives and moves and has its being in these sonnets.

My own first acquaintance with them was made under conditions the most favourable for intimacy. The little volume published in 1830 was the first publication I had seen by a man whom I knew ! And as the man in this instance was a familiar friend, companion, and coeval, in whom, and in all that proceeded from him, I took a most affectionate interest, it is needless to say how eagerly I went into his book, nor much to add how deeply I drank of it and how thoroughly I soon knew every line that it contained. Such things are of course. It is more to the purpose to say that, unlike so many objects of youthful admiration, that little volume has never, during the fifty years save one that have followed, lost for me any part of its charm : but I can take it up at any hour of any day, sure of finding all within it as fresh and bright as when I was an undergraduate.

The admiration, however, which it excited at its first appearance was by no means confined to personal friends. The critics of the press indeed, with one distinguished exception, were dull, and the sale was slow : for the measures that must be taken to give a

book by a new author a chance of getting into circu-
lation were not only not taken, they were not thought
of or imagined, either by Charles Turner himself or
any of us, his friends and allies. 'I have long ago
discovered,' wrote a printer of large experience in the
book trade—but this was long after—to a friend of
mine, 'that books are sold, not bought ;—that a clever
publisher can *plant* a large lot, at perhaps a small
reduction, on some special seller at Manchester or
Edinburgh, who will push off 100 or 500 copies, while
no ten men would have gone to purchase copies.'
If my own experience was not exceptionally unlucky,
ten men might have gone to the publisher of the
'Sonnets' to purchase copies, and come away with-
out them. For I went myself once on that errand
(thinking in my ignorance that what must otherwise
have been paid to the retail bookseller and his agents
would thereby be saved for the author), and found
considerable difficulty in making the shopmen under-
stand that they had any such book to sell ; though a
search in the warehouse brought it out.

In other ways its reception was far from dis-
couraging. Leigh Hunt in the 'Tatler' (though not
personally acquainted with either of the brothers)
welcomed it and Alfred Tennyson's first volume,
which came out nearly at the same time, with the
liveliest delight ; as superior to anything he had seen
'since the last volume of Keats ;' as books which
entitled their authors to 'take their stand at once
among the first poets of the day '—books in which the
readers of Spenser and Chaucer would at once find
themselves 'in a new district of their old territory,'

and 'feel, in turning the first leaf, as if they closed the portal behind them, and were left alone with nature and a new friend.' The margins of Coleridge's copy of the 'Sonnets' overflowed with applausive comments in his own handwriting ; and the private opinions generally of those whose attention was called to them carried encouragement quite enough to satisfy the aspirations of the most diffident and least praise-exacting of poets, whose heart was in his brother's progress and success very much more than in his own. And yet it so happened that that short out-burst of song was followed by a silence of many years, during which he not only published nothing, but hardly wrote anything. Inquiries by friends after new poems were answered by a few detached fragments—notes of casual thoughts, images, or similes—such as these following ; which I extracted from him one night, and wrote down in a note-book as he repeated them.

> Even the great Deluge, when its task was done,
> Threw up a rosy arch, and ebbed away.

> [Study of Gold Fish in a Glass Vase.]
> As though King Midas did the surface touch,
> Constraining the clear waters to their change,
> With shooting motions and quick trails of light,
> Now a rich girth, and then a narrow gleam,
> And now a shaft, and now a sheet of gold.[1]

---

[1] See p. 234, where some of the descriptive force is sacrificed to make room for the moral application.

As Memnon's statue, at the touch of morn,
Forewent its ingrained silence, and sent forth
A gentle orison to greet the sun.[1]

. . . . .

[The opening of the Tomb of Charlemagne.]
They rove the marble where the ancient king
Like one forespent with sacred study sate,
Robed like a king, but as a scholar pale.

. . . . .

Remorse
Hath struck her knotted roots into my heart,
To suck my hopes into her mighty stem.

It was on the same occasion, I think, that he re-
peated to me the sonnet on 'Some Humming-Birds
in a Glass Case,' which he published without much
alteration in his latest volume.[2] And there were four
lines,—a sonnet in themselves, though only an ejacu-
lation, and without any rhymes at all—which I heard
at some other time, either from himself or his brother,
and have a note of in the same book. He afterwards
found a place for them in a regular fourteen-liner ;[3]
where I should have admired them more if I had not
known them so long in their natural shape before
they were fitted into the frame. The poet, walking
about the wolds in autumn, speaks to himself.

Ah! woody hills, and autumn tints divine!
Ah! mournful eyes! Ah! sad poetic soul!
Ah! beauteous thoughts, with fatal sorrow trained
To twine for ever round this cumbered heart!

---

[1] See the beginning of a sonnet on the waking to song of
' the lesser children of the day—the window-flies,' p. 244; and
the conclusion of that on 'Modern Termini,' p. 161.

[2] P. 327. [3] P. 144.

At a later period of his occultation, he told me his
sonnet about the shadow of 'the lattice at sunrise,'[1]
and, if I recollect right, one or two more relating to
the sadder experiences of his life, which I remember
chiefly in connexion with his remark when I praised
one of them.   He had been much affected in reciting
it, and replied that he thought it was good, for he
'*knew* that it was true :' the only expression, by the
way, approaching to praise of anything of his own
that I can remember hearing him utter ; his habitual
feeling with regard to himself being that which is
expressed in his 'Sonnet to a Friend'[2]—

> My low deserts consist not with applause
> So kindly—when I fain would deem it so,
> My sad heart, musing on its proper flaws,
> Thy gentle commendation must forego.
>
> .   .   .   .   .   .
>
> Self-knowledge baulked self-love.

It was from the predominance of this feeling,
probably, that he fell into that long silence, broken
only by such snatches as I have set down, which made
his friends fear that he had lost his voice.   It could
not have been from disappointment at the reception
of his book by the 'general reader :' for one who was
content with so little, the recognition it met with
(which, properly estimated, was not a little) would
certainly have been encouragement enough.   It could
not have been from the paralysis or exhaustion of the
poetic faculty : his mind was as busy as ever, gather-
ing from all the sights and sounds of nature, within

---

[1] P. 149.   [2] P. 157.

and without, food for meditation, warning, gratitude,
delight, or consolation. It could not have been from
over-occupation in the business of his profession ;
which, lying always in a country parish, brought him
into daily contact with the very scenes and incidents
which made his fancy blossom. It could not have
been from any superstitious feeling, like that which
determined Moultrie to renounce verse-making ; be-
cause

> In sooth 'twas time at twenty-seven
> His muse should be the bride of heaven ;—

as if verse were a vanity too secular for a clergyman :
for Charles Turner employed his muse as the cham-
pion of his Church, and whatever may have been the
cause which suspended his poetical activity, we owe
its revival to his alarm at the intrusion of modern
criticism into the sacred precinct. 'The sonnet,' he
said, 'was his weapon.' Depression of mind by other
sorrows, of which he had a heavy burden to bear,
might be thought a more probable explanation, and it
had its effect, no doubt,[1]—were it not that this very
depression was the source of some of his finest
works :—

> He learned in suffering what he taught in song.

But the real cause of that long silence (as I was
told by one of his friends at the time—for our ways
in life parted soon after we both left college, and we

---

[1] 'The edge of thought was blunted by the stress
  Of the hard world ; my fancy had waxed dull,
  All nature seemed less nobly beautiful, —
  Robbed of her grandeur and her loveliness ;
  Methought the Muse within my heart had died.'—P. 145.

saw little of each other for many years) was a morbid apprehension that his poetry was not *original.* Morbid, I call it ; for I think it would be hard to find a poet whose distinctive originality is more clearly traceable in every line or half-line that he wrote. But his ideal was high, his opinion of himself low ; he was not stimulated to self-assertion by any disputes or jealousies—if he ever thought ill of anybody but himself (which I doubt), he never acted upon the thought :—in such cases a sensitive mind will turn to self-criticism and fall into delusions ; and as a foreign enemy is the best cure for internal dissension, it may well be that when he called in his genius to defend his creed, his old quarrel with it for want of originality was forgotten, and he consented to employ it again in its proper work.

Not that, in my opinion, its proper work lay in that warfare. In the last two-and-twenty sonnets of his second volume (published in 1864) the execution is masterly in its way. But serious arguments on questions of that kind cannot be discussed in stanzas of fourteen lines each ; and scornful denunciation of conclusions which remain unrefuted is only effective where your majority is overwhelming, and the question can be carried by acclamation. ' Turn him out ' may silence a troublesome auditor who sees that all the world is against him : but in the present condition of biblical criticism the only effect of contemptuous epithets is to flatter the hearts of those who use them, and provoke the contempt of those they are aimed at. No enemy will think the worse of himself for them, or the better of the cause which is so defended : no neutral will be moved by them at all. And it is the more pity that his zeal impelled him in this solitary instance into satirical invective, because if, instead of denouncing the questioners of ' our grand old faith,' ' our full-orbed creeds,' and ' our great dogmas,' he had only held up before them an image of what to him was real and vital in the faith itself, the picture would have been attractive ; and though it would not have extinguished their doubts, it would have won their sympathy. If the allowances—the reasonable allowances—which in the following sonnet are made for *some* among them had been extended to all, nothing would have been lost by the concession, and something might have been gained.

> I tax not all with this unmanly hate
> Of truth, for purer spirits stand without—
> Meek men of reverent purpose watch and wait,
> And gaze in sorrow from the land of doubt.
> Yes—gentle souls there be who hold apart
> And long in silence for the day of grace ;
> For deep in many a brave though bleeding heart
> There lurks a yearning for the Healer's face—
> A yearning to be free from hint and guess ;
> To take the blessings Christ is fain to give.[1]

Such as these, he hopes, may

> Push through these dark philosophies, and live.

So again in the ' recommendatory letter' for ' the Young Neologist at Bethlehem : '—

> Ye shepherds ! angels now ! who gladly heard
> That midnight Word of God, in music given
> Which told of Christ's Nativity, and stirred

---

[1] P. 169.

Your hearts with melodies from middle heaven ;
Tend this poor creedless youth through David's town !
Be ever near him with a silent spell,
And lead him to the spot where, floating down
Upon your watch, the choral blessing fell !
There charm away his false and flimsy lore,
And breathe into his soul your simple creed, &c.

This surely is a way of dealing with the subject
more likely to prevail than satirical pictures of 'bleak-
faced Neology, in cap and gown' (p. 167) ; of the
'Higher Criticism' bedaubing with ink the puffed
hand of sophistry ; 'striking its small penknife through
the Covenants '(p. 173); and blandly giving its 'foolish
blessing' to the Bible (p. 182) :—of the learned
critics, all agape to lure to their fancy-perch 'the
stately-soaring eagle of Saint John' (p. 174) ; or of the
white-robed Priest at Christmas standing (p. 176)

Forsworn—amid the faithful evergreens.

And if the professors of the 'higher criticism' will seek
' beyond these voices,'—strangely discordant from the
mouth of one incapable in any other relation of con-
tempt or harshness towards any creature—for the
substance of the faith which they are meant to en-
force, they will find nothing offensive in it, even
though they have a faith of their own which they like
better.   They will only find such doctrine as is ex-
pressed or implied in these passages that follow :—

The sorrowing manhood of the King of kings, .
The double nature, and the death of shame,
The tomb—the rising—are substantial things. —(p. 162.)

[1] P. 181.

> to succeed
> In that great race to Faith alone is given—
> On-looking Faith, whose object fires the will;
> And as the distance shrinks 'twixt earth and heaven,
> Glows with its motion, and bears forward still.—(p. 166.)

> When will the impugners of the Gospel claims
> The deep consistent likeness recognise
> Between His woes and glories ?   Living ties
> That bind in one His honours and His shames?
> For all coheres; His pangs and triumphs touch
> Each other, like the wings of Cherubim.
> Strange was His Birth—His death and rising such
> As to bear out that strangeness—and as much
> May well be said of dark Gethsemane,
> That sternest link in the great unity.—(p. 170.)

> O cruel conclave! where those murderers met;
> O vile night-market! where our Lord was sold
> Among the sad grey olives, in His sweat,
> Just risen from that awful prayer,—behold !
> They lead Him forth, the Victim long foretold,
> To climb, like Isaac, up the fated hill;
> And so God wrought Redemption.—(p. 171.)

> the deep grief
> Which all imaginative art would faint
> To express— the Angel's visit of relief,
> The God bowed earthward, like some mourning saint—
> They tone down all. . . .
> Not so the Church ! and tho' she needs must blush
> At her own feeble handling, yet alway,
> When she would paint her Master's darkest day,
> She takes the full-hued life-drop on her brush,
> And works in simple faith as best she may.—(p. 172.)

Surely it is not the reality of the crucifixion, or the significance of the 'sweat of anguish,' that the critics call in question ; and if they regard the sufferer as a

godlike man rather than a manlike God, it is not *they*
who make the sacrifice less awful to the human
imagination or the submission less sublime.

But though Charles Turner felt it a religious duty
to protest against inquiry into these things—*tantum
Religio potuit suadere*—his own real religion was that
of the Church universal ; the natural piety which,
like the rain and the sunshine, is vouchsafed alike to
the heterodox and the orthodox, to the critic who
desires to know the truth, and the believer who thinks
he knows already.   This religion is always with him,
and always expresses itself in forms which require at
most the occasional translation of a technical phrase
to engage the sympathy of every man who has any
religion at all.

I have spoken of his management of the sonnet
in point of *form*. For the *matter* of it, and the
management of that, we may gather his ideas from an
allusion to it[1] in relation to the 'quick gleam that
rides upon the gossamer'—a favourite object, which
with its 'shy returns and beautiful escapes' was so
fertile to him of fine suggestions :—

> whose buoyant thread
> Is as the sonnet, poising one bright thought,
> That moves but does not vanish! borne along
> Like light—a golden drift through all the song.

In another place he finds in the action of sunrise
upon the dew an illustration of 'the process of com-
position.'

---

[1] P. 308.

Oft in our fancy an uncertain thought
Hangs colourless, like dew on bents of grass,
Before the morning o'er the field doth pass;
But soon it glows and brightens; all unsought
A sudden glory flashes through the dream;
Our purpose deepens, and our wit grows brave,
The thronging hints a richer utterance crave,
And tongues of fire approach the new-won theme:
A subtler process now begins—a claim
Is urged for order, a well-balanced scheme
Of words and numbers, a consistent aim;
The dew dissolves before the warming beam;
But that fair thought consolidates its flame,
And keeps its colours, hardening to a gem.[1]

Cultivated in this spirit, ' the sonnet's humble plot of ground' (the motto which he chose for his earliest volume) supplied him with work enough ; and the same modesty which resisted all persuasion to venture a flight beyond its limit confined him for his subject-matter among the objects with which he was most familiar. Nor was this to be regretted. For nothing in nature, animate or inanimate, could be so common, or to ordinary eyes so insignificant, but his fine observation, tender thought, and pathetic humour would find matter in it for the imagination, the fancy, the heart, or the conscience ; and few readers possessed of any of the four can wander leisurely with him through these little volumes without finding that a walk in an English country parish may be as full of fine surprises as an unexplored land in another hemisphere.

---

[1] P. 147.

C

Not that his meditations or his interests were confined to his parish. He was a scholar, a reader, and, though not a great traveller, he had seen strange lands. His memory was well stored with classical imagery. The great events and great biographies of the past, the struggles of the nations and the victories of humanity in the present, and the hidden future of his country and his race, filled him with emotion, and inspired strains which will probably take place hereafter, many of them, among the memorable utterances of our time. He was always original ; his thoughts and language, both, were always his own, whether they had been used by others or not ; and his range was wide. Achilles shouting from the trench ; Philoctetes returning to the war with the arrows of 'the twelve-fold labourer ;' Ulysses relieved in his shipwreck by the 'brave-eyed pity' of Nausicaa ; Alexander the Great at Babylon ; Julian building on the site of the Temple ; the blush of Constantine on entering the Council at Nice ; the lachrymatory brought from the Roman tomb, with the dream which it suggested ; the old Roman shield fished up out of the Thames ; the White Horse of Westbury, which he 'dreamed into living will '—

> He neighed, and straight the chalk poured down the hill ;
> He shook himself, and all beneath was stoned :
> Hengist and Horsa shouted o'er my sleep
> Like fierce Achilles ; while that storm-blanched horse
> Sprang to the van of all the Saxon force,
> And pushed the Britons to the western deep—

Mary of Scotland and Elizabeth ; Nelson driving among the French ships 'the yeast of his fierce voyage ;' Charlotte Corday, with maiden's hand blood-stained from her noble crime—these, and many more of the kind, were as familiar to his imagination as the little Sophys and Katies, with their wooden spades and laurel crowns, in whose innocent enjoyments he took so much delight ; and how deep the impressions were which such things made upon him, we may learn from his lines on a picture of Armida and Rinaldo,[1] which I shall quote entire, as telling us something of the early culture of the imagination which was to bear this fruit.

> Dear is that picture for my childhood's sake, —
> The man asleep, so near to love or harm ;
> The wingèd boy, that stays Armida's arm,
> The siren-girl, all hushed, lest he awake ;
> While, in the background of that pictured tale,
> Sown with enchanted herbs, and clad with gloom,
> A sombre eminence o'erlooks the vale,
> A purple hill, where all my dreams found room :
> 'Tis strange with how few touches of a brush
> That painter's hand supplied, in life's fresh dawn,
> The mystic thoughts I loved ! sweet thoughts ! deep-drawn,
> Far-destined : cherished still without a blush ;
> Deep-drawn—from God's own founts of mystery ;
> Far-destined—for my soul must ever be.

But though the imagery derived from books and pictures retained its hold and took new life under his treatment, it is in the kindly human interest which he infuses into everything that he looks upon or thinks of, that his special and peculiar originality is most

---

[1] P. 198.

C 2

conspicuous. Not merely everything that feels, or moves, or grows, but everything that has a meaning or a function in the world, he endues and regards with an affectionate sympathy, so tender and so catching that it seems hard to refuse it the rights of a fellow-creature. Wordsworth's bird's nest filled with snow would have been for him, not so much a thing resembling and recalling the condition of a forsaken lover's heart, as a thing with a heart of its own, suffering its own sorrow. He would have made you feel, not for yourself or your friend, whose case it reminds you of, but for the nest itself—left by all its nurslings to starve.

When he hears the buoy-bell ringing on the shoal,[1] he feels grateful, not to those who anchored it there, but to the poor thing itself that has to perform the duty.

> How like the leper, with his own sad cry
> Enforcing his own solitude, it tolls !
> That lonely bell set in the rushing shoals
> To warn us from the place of jeopardy !
> O friend of man ! sore-vext by ocean's power,
> The changing tides wash o'er thee day by day,
> Thy trembling mouth is filled with bitter spray,
> Yet still thou ringest on from hour to hour ;
> High is thy mission, though thy lot is wild, &c.

When he hears the beats of the hydraulic ram in the field,[2] he saddens at the lonely lot of the imprisoned engine, plying its dull pulses night and day in the darkness.

---

[1] P. 108.   [2] P. 281.

The willow-twig [1] that he had stuck in the ground
to prop a rose, grows up into a beautiful tree, a

> mighty bower,—
> My summer tent, my waving canopy,—

but it had overborne its nursling, and the remem-
brance will not let it rest.

> Methinks each child of earth some sorrow knows
> Akin to ours : long since, that infant rose
> Drooped ere its time and bowed its head to die,
> While thou hast soared aloft, to toss and sigh.

The sunbeam [2] which, as he walks in the forest
glade on the dark morning, full of sad thoughts, enters
at the other end,

> And runs to meet him through the yielding shade

is welcomed

> As one who in the distance sees a friend,
> And smiling hurries to him,

with tears of delight.

In his lighter moods, the same fellow-feeling
expresses itself in a kind of affectionate playfulness.
We knew from Milton that Time was a thief ; but the
silver-voiced timepiece in the poet's study,[3] not con-
tent with stealing his hours, seems to twit him
pleasantly with his loss.

> My clock's a mocking thief, who steals my coin,
> Then, counting up the sum, as if to say,
> ' How many precious pieces I purloin,
> One, two, three, four '—trips daintily away.

---

[1] P. 306.   [2] P. 146.   [3] P. 307.

The scarecrow, standing in the field after the harvest is over, in hat and coat, with outstretched arms—familiar to us all as a somewhat comic character—is to him [1] an object of affectionate pity :—

> Couldst thou but push a hand from out thy sleeve !
> Or smile on me !   But ah ! thy face is nil !
> The stubbles darken round thee, lonely one !
> And man has left thee, all this dreary term,
> No mate beside thee--far from social joy ;
> As some poor clerk survives his ruined firm,
> And in a napless hat, without employ,
> Stands in the autumn of his life alone.

The lot of the outgrown rocking-horse [2] is less forlorn ; for while he stands in his corner of the hall he retains a kind of personality, and is recognised as one of the household.   But what he *feels*, when

> Eustace and Edith too
> Ride living steeds : she leans her dainty whip
> Across his smooth-worn flank, and feels him dip
> Beneath the pressure, while she dons a shoe,
> Or lifts a glove, and thinks, ' My childhood's gone ! '
> While the young statesman, with high hopes possest,
> Lays a light hand upon his yielding crest
> And rocks him vacantly, and passes on—

is known only to himself and his poet.

> Oh, give him kindly greeting, man and maid,
> And pat him, as you pass, with friendly hands,
> In that dim window where disused he stands,
> While o'er him breaks the lime-walk's flickering shade.
> No provender, no mate, no groom has he :
> His stall and pasture is your memory.

---

[1] P. 305.   [2] P. 205.

To one who feels thus towards these creatures of
the joiner and the mechanist it is needless to say that
every living thing is a friend. And though in follow-
ing nature into all her nooks and corners he must
have made acquaintance with some of her creatures
that are ugly, offensive, aggressive, or otherwise in-
tolerable to man, he has no quarrel with any. If he
knows any ill of them he says nothing about it ; and
so delicately does he touch upon the 'viewless
quarry' of his favourite swallow, and other innocent
carnivora, that, were it not for the death of Minnie's
dove by the stroke of a kite,[1] we should hardly
imagine that Nature, in the absence of man, allowed
such things to be done. Of man's doings in that kind
we have a penitent and touching record in the ' Plea
of the shot Swallow.'[2]

> In Teos once, bedewed with odours fine,
> The happy dove slept on his master's lyre.
> A little homeless swallow clings to mine,
> A spirit-bird —he looks for something higher
> Than songs and odours : pity and remorse
> He claims —an elegy of words and tears.

It was a swallow shot by himself when he was a
boy, and remembered with remorse all the days of
his life. The single really noxious creature to which
I find any allusion in these volumes is a human rogue
who trades in the plunder of widows and orphans,
and fails to profit by a chance of amendment which
nature thrusts upon him. For having taken a walk in
the country to enjoy himself after concluding a

---

[1] P. 204. [2] P. 235.

fraudulent bargain, he dreams at night that a running brook has washed the ink out of the newly signed title-deeds. But the horror of the thought wakes him. He returns to his craft, and the story of the 'Rogue's Nightmare'[1] remains to show that there was one living thing for which Charles Turner could feel neither hope nor pity. But perhaps he had only read of him.

Of Nature, when left to herself, his representation is perhaps a little too indulgent. But a poet is not a statistician. It was not his business to make an exhaustive report of everything that is permitted on the earth. He had a full right to make his own selection—to seek the flowers that yield the honey ; and what he sought in nature was whatever is beautiful, and pure, and innocent, and lovable. He sought it everywhere, in the smallest as in the largest objects ; and found it in everything, from the dewdrop to the full rainbow ; from 'the hedge-row's flowery breast of lacework' to

> the mighty landscape stretched
> To the far hills through green and azure grades ;

from the 'glimmer in the watery rut,' revealing 'a star—in heaven, yet by his side,' to Orion, soaring

> from out some snowy cloud
> Which held the frozen breath of land and sea,
> Yet broke and severed as the wind grew loud ;

from the 'bright eye and innocent dismay' of the

---

[1] P. 208.

gold-crested wren, when caught to be let out of the
window, to the wheeling eagle—

> An arrow feathered with two mighty vans,
> That soars and stoops at will, and broadly scans
> The woods and waters with a living sight.

It would be easy to fill pages with happy descrip-
tions of the familiar objects of English landscape, as
seen under all varieties of season and weather ; but
his enjoyment of pure nature, and its healing influence
on his mind, will be better seen perhaps in a single
picture of a summer daybreak, represented as the
occasion of his recovery from a state of mental de-
pression. The opening lines, in which that state is
described, I have already quoted.[1] Here is the
cure :—

> Methought the Muse within my heart had died ;
> Till, late, awakened at the break of day,
> Just as the East took fire and doffed its grey,
> The rich preparatives of light I spied.
> But one sole star—none other anywhere—
> A wild-rose odour from the fields was borne ;
> The lark's mysterious joy filled earth and air,
> And from the wind's top met the hunter's horn ;
> The aspen trembled wildly : and the morn
> Breathed up in rosy clouds, divinely fair !

With a nature so affectionate, and its affections so
engaged to the 'old ruralities' of his boyhood—the
heath-bell lingering in the enclosed moorland—the
'slip-shouldered flail still busy on the poor man's

---

[1] See note, p. 11.

threshing-floor '—the unshorn hedge-row surviving its cropped and stunted neighbours—

> The thatch and houseleek, where old Alice lives,
> With her old herbal, trusting every page—

and the spinning-wheel humming far down in the lone valley [1]—it might have been thought that the railway, the viaduct, and the steam-engine, would be resented as unwelcome intruders, fatal to poetry and the picturesque. But he was too true a poet for that. Sorry as he was to see the old friends departing, his heart was large enough to welcome and appreciate the great new-comers. The

> trembling in the sea-girt isle,
> Where ' Hercules ' or mighty ' Samson ' trod,
> Heavy and swift ; [2]

the ' vast mechanics ' of the Barmouth sea-bridge,[3] with ' all its great crossbeams, and clamps, and ties '— told of the greatness of England. The ' brawling and hushing ' of the distant railway,[4] making sensible the universal stillness of nature, while ' the shadow of our travelling earth ' hung on the moon, supplies him with the most picturesque incident in his description of the lunar eclipse. And the contemplation of the ' steam threshing-machine with the straw-carrier '[5] raises him into the highest region of poetry.

> Flush with the pond the lurid furnace burned
> At eve, while smoke and vapour filled the yard :
> The gloomy winter sky was dimly starred,
> The fly-wheel with a mellow murmur turned ;

---

[1] P. 302.   [2] P. 132.   [3] P. 275.
[4] P. 247.   [5] P. 242, 3.

While, ever rising on its mystic stair
In the dim light, from secret chambers borne,
The straw of harvest, severed from the corn,
Climbed, and fell over, in the murky air.
I thought of mind and matter, will and law,
And then of him who set his stately seal
Of Roman words on all the forms he saw
Of old-world husbandry. *I* could but feel
With what a rich precision *he* would draw
The endless ladder and the booming wheel!

Did any seer of ancient time forebode
This mighty engine, which we daily see
Accepting our full harvests, like a god,
With clouds about his shoulders,—it might be
Some poet-husbandman, some lord of verse,
Old Hesiod, or the wizard Mantuan
Who catalogued in rich hexameters
The Rake, the Roller, and the mystic Van;
Or else some priest of Ceres, it might seem,
Who witnessed, as he trod the silent fane,
The notes and auguries of coming change,—
Of other ministrants in shrine and grange,—
The sweating statue, and her sacred wain
Low-booming with the prophecy of steam!

All dishes cannot be made to suit all palates.
The merit of the entertainment is decided by the
impression left on the whole party, when each has
helped himself to what he liked best. In a long
poem each reader finds this or that part comparatively
uninteresting, but his final judgment represents his
general impression of the whole. In a volume of
sonnets, on the contrary,—as in a collection of
apophthegms, anecdotes, or witticisms,—each piece is
presented separately to each guest to be tasted and

pronounced upon ; and thus the number of the *dis-*
tasteful, which in a continuous work would have been
merely passed by, is observed and remembered, and
makes part of the general impression.

Charles Turner's habit of taking for his theme any
real incident that took his fancy or touched his feel-
ings in life or book, insured endless variety of matter,
and unfailing sincerity of treatment : but being united
with a simplicity so childlike and a sympathy so con-
fiding, it dignified with song many matters in which
' the wise world ' may see little to interest or affect it.
Substituting the love which is associated with child-
hood for that which the Duke in ' Twelfth Night '
speaks of in describing the clown's song—

> It is silly sooth,
> And dallies with the innocence of love,
> Like the old age —

the description may be applied to many of these
sonnets, and by some critics it will be applied in
censure.   But however they may agree in thinking
that the collection would be improved by taking out
those they do not care for, I suspect that if the choice
were referred to a committee large enough to be
representative, those proposed for omission by one
would generally prove to be special favourites with
another. It is better therefore that each reader
should make the selection for himself, taking what he
likes, leaving what he does not like, and making no
complaint as long as he gets enough.

In the passages which I have quoted, I have
sought not so much for what I like best myself, or

imagine may be thought best by the general reader, as
for illustrations of the writer's peculiar character,
gifts, and humours ; for what strikes me as most
characteristic in him when compared with others.   If
I had room to follow him from inanimate through the
various regions of animated nature,—the world of
insects, birds, beasts, little children,—the 'path
through hamlets in the eve or prime '—the loves,
joys, sorrows, and consolations of humble life ;—the
sick-room, the death-bed, the death-smile,—

> prelude of immortal peace
> Now that the storm of life has reached its end—

the poetic vision of bodily resurrection—

> on high
> A record lives of thine identity :
> Thou shalt not lose one charm of lip or eye ;
> The hues and liquid lights shall wait for thee,
> And the fair tissues, wheresoe'er they be—

the aspirations after a truer brotherhood and a purer
ideal among the nations of the earth—and the
welcome accorded to all great examples and all
material means which promise to help in bringing it
on,—it would be seen that whatever we take to be
the distinguishing mark of the true poet,—whether
imaginative sympathy with nature, as Wordsworth
used to maintain, or application of moral ideas to
questions concerning man and nature and human
life, as Mr. Matthew Arnold rules it, or the power of
casting beautiful thoughts into forms which are ac-
cepted at once and remembered for ever, which I
take to be the common opinion—we have a true poet

here ; and one who among the candidates for immortality (which is no respecter of size or quantity) is entitled to a high place. But a claim of this extent could not be made good by extracts in any moderate number. For its justification I must be content with an appeal to the entire collection ; coupled only with this caution ; that as all works are remembered in succeeding generations by what is best in them and most enduring, the critics in the present generation who aspire to predict their future must judge them on the same principle, on pain of being themselves remembered (if remembered at all) only as false prophets.

The present volume contains all his sonnets, published and unpublished, and is itself the most appropriate record of a life of studious privacy, the *events* of which, lying almost entirely within the little round of duties indicated in the ' Pastor's prayer,'[1] supply no matter for the biographer. The new church and the new church clock were perhaps the most memorable of them—the annual school feast[2] the most stirring and picturesque.

> The feast is o'er—the music and the stir—
> The sound of bat and ball, the mimic gun ;
> The lawn grows darker, and the setting sun
> Has stolen the flash from off the gossamer,
> And drawn the midges westward ; youth's glad cry—
> The smaller children's fun-exacting claims,
> Their merry raids across the graver games,
> Their ever-crossing paths of restless joy,

---

[1] P. 323.   [2] P. 321.

Have ceased—and, ere a new feast day shall shine,
Perchance my soul to other worlds may pass;
Another head in childhood's cause may plot,
Another pastor muse in this same spot,
And the fresh dews, that gather on the grass
Next morn, may gleam on every track but mine.

But the interest which his life has for others lies not in its incidents, but in the man himself—his mind and spirit. And of that there will remain in this volume an unconscious record, so full and true, that I doubt whether those who knew him best could add anything material to the image which an attentive reader will form of him as he reads,—except the assurance that it does not represent an idealised character, such as poets and prosers alike are apt to put on for the business of their imaginary lives, but his real character in his real life, as he appeared to all who knew him. 'He felt kindness'—so one of the most intimate friends of his later as well as his earlier years wrote to me the day after his death— 'and had deep gratitude for it, almost more than any one I ever knew : an unkind word or thought was to him almost inconceivable.' Of such a character and such a life, endowed as, it was by nature, through its great gift of music, with power to speak for itself, his own works are the fittest memorial.

His monument shall be his gentle verse,
Which eyes not yet created shall o'erread,
And tongues to be his being shall rehearse,
When all the breathers of this world are dead.

JAMES SPEDDING.

SONNETS

SONNETS PUBLISHED IN 1830.

[The first fifty sonnets which follow were published at Cambridge in 1830, in the author's college-days. Though most of them were republished in his later volumes, and many with material alterations, it has been thought best to present them here in their original form, as the genuine produce of early youth, rather than as modified afterwards under the influence of ideas and experiences to which he was then a stranger. Where, indeed, the object of the change has been merely to remove some defect in composition, which he might have observed and corrected at any time of his life, the later reading has been taken into the text; but where it extends to the thought, or sentiment, or moral significance, it has been remitted to the notes, as not properly belonging to the stage of mental progress which that part of the volume represents. In such cases the text exhibits the reading of the earliest edition.

The notes signed S.T.C. were found on the margin of the copy in which S. T. Coleridge read them at the time,—written in his own hand. There were also marks indicating the passages which he particularly liked. These are referred to in the footnotes as ' Coleridge's mark.']

TO MY SISTER MARY.

Sister, accept these lays ; as yet I ween
No lay but mine has open'd with thy name,
I would I were a bard of mightier fame,
Then would this tribute of more price have been,
And thou had'st worn a costlier pledge, in sign
Of my deep love !   My name is all unknown,
And, daring not to venture forth alone,
It fondly seeks companionship of thine ;
And thou dost love me more than to believe
Thy brother's song can furnish shame to thee ;
Critics ! be your dispraise from harshness free,
And scornful gibe, nor give her cause to grieve,
For, if ye sternly say I cannot sing,
My sister's name is on a shaméd thing !

I.

THE ÆOLIAN HARP.

O take that airy harp from out the gale,
Its troubles call from such a distant bourne,
Now that the wind has wooed it to its tale
Of bygone bliss, that never can return ;
Hark ! with what dreamy sadness it is swelling !
How sweet it falls, unwinding from the breeze !
Disordered music, deep and tear-compelling,
Like siren-voices pealing o'er the seas.[1]
Nay, take it not, for now my tears are stealing,
But when it brake upon my mirthful hour,
And spake to joy of sorrow past the healing,
I shrank beneath the soft subduing power ;
Nay, take it not ; replace it by my bower—
The soul can thrill with no diviner feeling.

---

[1] These four lines marked by S.T.C.

II.

THE KISS OF BETROTHAL.

When lovers' lips from kissing disunite
With sound as soft as mellow fruitage breaking,
They loathe to leave what was so sweet in taking,
So fraught with breathless magical delight ;
The scent of flowers is long before it fade,
Long dwells upon the gale the Vesper-tone,
Far floats the wake the lightest skiff has made,
The closest kiss, when once imprest, is gone ;
What marvel, then, that each so closely kisseth ?
Sweet is the fourfold touch, the living seal—
What marvel, then, with sorrow each dismisseth
This thrilling pledge of all they hope and feel ?
While on their lingering steps the shadows steal,
And each true heart beats as the other wisheth.[1]

---

[1] In the original edition the last six lines stood thus :

'What marvel then that youth so fondly kisses,
That deep and long he prints the ardent seal !
What marvel then with sorrow he dismisses
The thrilling pledge of trustful hearts and leal !
While eyes look into eyes, and none represses
With meddling words the passion they reveal !

III.

PERSEVERANCE.

On, on, in firm progression, sure and slow,
More scorning hindrance, as ye meet it more ;
Surmounting what ye cannot thorough go,
And forcing what ye fail in climbing o'er ;
Soon shall ye gaze upon the bliss attained,
And worth attainment fourfold as severe ;
The glorious meed for zealous souls ordained,
Shall shine upon you, palpable and clear ;
Then when the starry coronal of Fame
Shall gird your brows, all-perdurably bright ;
When ye have seen the solitary flame,
That burns upon the solitary height,
Ye will not, then, your daily cares misname
As toil—well spent, for rapture to requite !

IV.

TO THE NIGHTINGALE.

O honey-throated warbler of the grove !
That in the glooming woodland art so proud
Of answering thy sweet mates in soft or loud,
Thou dost not own a note we do not love ;
The moon is o'er thee, laying out the lawn
In mighty shadows—but the western skies
Are kept awake, to see the sun arise,
Though earth and heaven would fain put back the
    dawn ! [1]
While, wandering for the dreams such seasons give,
With lonely steps, and many a pause between,
The lover listens to thy songs unseen ;
And if, at times, the pure notes seem to grieve,
Why lo ! he weeps himself, and must believe
That sorrow is a part of what they mean ! [2]

---

[1] In the original edition :
                    ' and the twilight skies
    Imbued with their unutterable dyes,
    A thousand hues from summer sources drawn.'

[2] In the original edition :
    ' With lonely steps thro' this transcendant scene,
    The poet weeps for joys that fled yestreen
    And staid not here to bless this purple eve,
    Too lately fled, and brought him here to grieve
    In passionate regret for what hath been.'

V.

TO THE LARK.

And am I up with thee, light-hearted minion?
Who never dost thine early flight forego,
Catching for aye upon thy gamesome pinion
What was to fill some lily's cup below,
The matin dew-fall?   What is half so thrilling
As thy glad voice i' th' argent prime of light?
Whether in grassy nest, when thou art billing,
Or thus aloft and mocking human sight?
Peace dwells with thee for ever—not the peace
Of cool reflection,[1] but redundant glee,
And with such vocal token of wild ease
Thou dost reveal thy proud immunity
From mortal care, that thou perforce must please:
Fair fall thy rapid song, sweet bird, and thee!

---

[1] '*With this sentence excepted (and it may be easily altered by substituting a positive and potentiative attribute of Peace for this somewhat smile-worthy truism in the negative), this V., me judice, is among the best sonnets in our language.*'—*S. T. C.*

This sonnet ('slightly altered') was included among those published in 1864. 'Morning shower-drops' was substituted for 'matin dew-fall' (out of respect, probably, for the theory of dew) and in deference apparently to Coleridge's criticism, ll. 7-10 were replaced by:

'Just risen from the nest where thou wert billing
A moment since, and with thy mate in sight,
Joy dwells with thee for ever—extasy—
Beyond the murmuring bliss of doves or bees.'

The first six have Coleridge's mark.

VI.

THE OCEAN.

The Ocean, at the bidding of the Moon,
For ever changes with his restless tide ;
Flung shoreward now, to be regather'd soon
With kingly pauses of reluctant pride,
And semblance of return.   Anon from home
He issues forth again, high ridged and free ;
The gentlest murmur of his seething foam,[3]
Like armies whispering where great echoes be !
Oh ! leave me here upon this beach to rove,
Mute listener to that sound so grand and lone—
A glorious sound, deep-drawn and strongly thrown,
And reaching those on mountain heights above ;
To British ears, as who shall scorn to own,
A tutelar fond voice, a Saviour-tone of love ![1]

---

[1] '*A noble sonnet.   But the last distich is inferior to my*
    "*And Ocean 'mid his uproar wild*
    Speaks safety to his Island child."—*Ode on dep. y.*

'(1) *I notice this only because it is too inferior for the resemblance.   The parenthesis is weak and of an alien tone of feeling :* a μετάβασις εἰς ἄλλο γένος, *though I admit not* εἰς ἕτερον. *But it is a noble strain*, non obstante.   [*In the last line*, dele "fond."]

'(2) *Might I recommend Mr. T. to substitute* (*for the lines beginning* "*Mute listener*," ' *&c.*):
    "*To that lone sound mute listener and alone,*
    And yet a sound of commune, strongly thrown,
    That meets the pine-grove on the cliffs above." '—*S.T.C.*

The first eight lines have Coleridge's mark.

(3) Altered to
    ' The seething hiss of his tumultuous foam.'

VII.

LOVE OF HOME.

A REJOINDER.

Hence ! with your jeerings petulant and low ;
My love of Home no circumstance can shake ;
Too ductile for the change of place to break,
And far too passionate for thee to know ;
I and yon sycamore have grown together,
How on yon slope the shifting sunsets lie,
None know like me and mine ; and, tending hither,
Flows the strong current of my memory ;
From that same flower-bed, ever dear to me,
I learn'd how marigolds [1] do bloom and fade ;
And from the grove, which skirts this garden-glade,
I had my earliest thoughts of Love and Spring ;
Thou wott'st not how the heart of man is made ;
I learn from thee what change the world can bring.

(1) Altered to
    ' I learn'd how all fair things do bloom and fade.'

VIII.

TO ———

How can the sweetness of a gentle mind
Pall on thy spirit ? say, it is not so ;
Her eyes are mournful and her sorrows flow,
For that she fears her hands have fail'd to bind
The tie of mutual wishes round thy heart ; [1]
Thy faith was given, thy promise made a part
Of the pure office which confirm'd her thine ;
Oh, do not thou annul that rite divine,
Nor bid such promise swell the tinsel-mart
Of empty shows, unmeaning types and vain—
But teach thy wife to nurse her hopes again
In love returning, never to depart ;
For nothing festers like a broken vow,
Which wrecks another's peace and blights another's
    brow.

---

[1] The first five lines are marked by S.T.C.

IX.

Vexation waits on passion's changeful glow,
But th' intellect may rove a thousand ways
And yet be calm while fluctuating so ;
The dew-drop shakes not to its shifting rays
And transits of soft light—be bold to choose
This never satiate freedom of delight
Before the fiery bowl and red carouse,
And task for joy thy soul's majestic might ;
So for the sensual will be rarer need,
So will thy mind a giant force assume,
Strong as the center of the deep Maelstroom
When flung into the calm of sightless speed : [1]
So wilt thou scorn on lowlier aims to feed,
And go in glory to a sage's tomb !

---

[1] *'A noble image, but obscurely and inadequately, or rather unprecisely, conveyed. Master Shakspeare has something (to answer) for that word "sightless"—used indifferently, now as unseeing, now as unseeable.—S.T.C.*

'P.S. I know of no adequate compensation for the mischief of an equivocal term.'—S.T.C.

This sonnet (of which lines 5–12 have Coleridge's mark) was rewritten—for other reasons, apparently, than deference to his criticism, though his objection is incidentally avoided—and in the volume published in 1873 reappeared in the following form :

SCIENCE AND FAITH.

Vexation waits on Passion's changeful glow,
But the Intellect may shed its wholesome rays
O'er many a theme, yet never work thee woe !
The sun is calm, while with his genial blaze
He makes all nature bright; be bold to choose
This still, concenter'd, permanent, delight,

X.

TO ——

I have a circlet of thy sunny hair,
And 'tis, I wot, a blessing to mine eyes—
For gentle, happy thoughts are sworn to rise
Whene'er I view it softly folded there,
Lifeless and listless,[1] like a treasure's key,
Unwitting of the dreams it doth compel
Of gems and gold piled high in secret cell,
Too royal for a vulgar gaze to see !
If they were stolen, the key might never tell ;
If thou wert dead, what should thy ringlet say ?
It shows the same, betide thee ill or well,
Smiling on earth, or shrouded in decay !
And were cold winter with thee, Isabel,
I might be smiling here on blossoms of thy May !

Before the fiery bowl and red carouse,
Nor dull with wanton acts thine inner sight ;
So for the sensual shall be rarer need,
So shall a mighty onward work be done ;
But oh ! let Faith and Reverence take the lead,
Test all half-knowledge with a jealous heed,
Nor set thy Science jarring with thy Creed ;
Each has its orbit round Truth's central Sun !

[1] '*Languid and listless I understand. Doubtless so I might have interpreted "lifeless," but for the "key," which fixes it in the primary sense. I would not have inserted this sonnet into so small a volume. The feeling seems to me fluttering and unsteady, pouncing and skimming on a succession of truisms.*'—*S. T. C.*

In the volume published in 1873 this sonnet is inserted under the title of 'The Traveller and his Wife's Ringlet'; the first five and the last two lines being altered, as follows :

XI.

A SUMMER TWILIGHT.

It is a Summer gloaming, balmy-sweet,
A gloaming brighten'd by an infant moon,
Fraught with the fairest light of middle June ;
The lonely garden echoes to my feet,
And hark ! O hear I not the gentle dews,
Fretting the silent forest in his sleep ?
Or does the stir of housing insects creep
Thus faintly on mine ear ? Day's many hues
Waned with the paling light and are no more,
And none but drowsy pinions beat the air :
The bat is hunting softly by my door,
And, noiseless as the snow-flake, leaves his lair ;
O'er the still copses flitting here and there,
Wheeling the self-same circuit o'er and o'er.[1]

'I have a circlet of thy sunny hair,
A light from home, a blessing to mine eyes ;
Though grave and mournful thoughts will often rise,
As I behold it mutely glistening there,
So still, so passive ! like a treasure's key, &c.

. . . . . .

It cannot darken for dead Isabel,
Nor blanch, if thy young head grew white to-day !'

[1] '*This (and indeed a large proportion of these sonnets)
stands between Wordsworth's and Southey's, and partakes of the
excellencies of both.*

'"*Gloaming,*" *Scotch or English ! At all events, I would
have spelt the word like an Englishman, "gloaming."*'—S.T.C.

This was included in the volume published in 1868, under
the title of 'Small Tableaux' ; 'gloaming' being altered to

XII.

O be thou keen to guess when Flattery's near !
His face is not the shadow of his heart :
The court is all for lucre like the mart,
And fraught with perils that a king should fear—
Trust not the flatterer's hollow sympathy :
For should'st thou fathom that dishonest sound,
The line would rise with noisome clays hung round
And not the fruitful loam of love for thee :
O ill-starred royalty !   Love's balmy sighs
Where Truth breathes on us from her sweetest shrine—
The access to all pure delights and ties—
Say, are they less the peasant's lot than thine ?
Beyond the shepherd's bliss thou canst not rise ;
And many snares to steal ev'n that combine.[1]

'twilight.'   The other alterations have been received into the text.   The whole of it, as first printed, was distinguished by Coleridge's approving mark.

   [1] '*That Tennyson possesses poetic taste, with both the feeling ana the plastic power of a Poet (= the poetic Bildungstrieb), is to me evident.   Whether he will be a great Poet, a Poet, is the same question as whether he will be a Philosopher and pure from the world.*

   '*And T. must not be very angry with me if I ask him* sotto voce *whether this XII. was not interpolated by his grandmother. Alas! the Heir Apparent is not more exposed to Flattery than Peasants and Dickons.*'—*S. T. C.*

   In the volume published in 1873, this sonnet was inserted, with some alterations and the title 'To a Young King.'   'All for lucre,' in the third line, is changed to 'shrewd and selfish,' and for the last six lines the following are substituted :

XIII.

No trace is left upon the vulgar mind
By shapes which form upon the poet's thought
In instant symmetry : all eyes are blind
Save his, for ends of lower vision wrought ;
Think'st thou, if Nature wore to every gaze
Her noble beauty and commanding power,
Could harsh and ugly doubt withstand the blaze
Or front her Sinai presence for an hour?
The seal of Truth is beauty—when the eye
Sees not the token, can the mission move?
The brow is veiled that should attach the tie
And lend the magic to the voice of Love :
What wonder then that doubt is ever nigh
Urging such spirits on to mock and to deny?[1]

Such are thy dangers ! but thy loves and joys
Are not more sweet than any shepherd-boy's ;
The access to all pure delights and ties
Is free to peasant stock, or kingly line ;
Beyond the common bliss thou can'st not rise,
And royal troubles and restraints are thine.

[1] ' " *The seal of Truth is Beauty.*"

' *I admire this sonnet—but I doubt whether the converse would not be at least equally just, viz. that the deadness to Truth occasions the blindness to Beauty.*'—*S. T. C.*

In the volume published in 1873, this sonnet is reproduced in a shape, and with a moral, entirely different. In its altered form, it belongs to another period of the author's life ; and,

XIV.

AUTUMN.

The softest shadows mantle o'er his form,
And the curved sickle in his grasp appears,
Glooming and brightening ; while a wreath of ears
Circles his sallow brow, which th' angry storm
Gusts down at intervals ; about him stray
The volant sweets o' the trailing mignonette,
And odours vague, that haunt the year's decay ;
The crush of leaves is heard beneath his feet,
Mixt, as he onward goes, with softer sound,
As tho' his heel were sinking into snows :
Full soon a sadder landscape opens round,
With, here and there, a latter-flowering rose,
Child of the Summer hours, though blooming here
Far down the vista of the fading year.

---

like the last, should be classed with the concluding sonnets of
the volume published in 1864.

TO ————

FAITH AND FREE-THINKING.

No trace is left upon that callous mind
By truths, that form on thy susceptive thought
In instant symmetry ; thy mate is blind,
A smart, free-thinking sophist, pledg'd to nought ;
Is he not blind, the man who rashly dares
To strut about a realm of mystery ?
Who carries up his small philosophy
Into the heights of Zion, and prepares
A lecture on his trespass ? To a heart
So brazed with wisdom, canst thou hope to prove

E

XV.

The foot of Time so soundless never pass'd
As when sweet fancy wove her magic thralls—
Go, mourner, to the Muses, haste thee, haste,
And bring thy griefs where Peter's shadow falls
To heal thee in his passing : [1] call for aid
Of joy, that quenches being and its gall—
Sad ! that the consciousness of Life must fade
Before the bliss it yields be felt at all :
We cannot sit, inertly calm'd, to hear
The silence broken by the step of life ;
We must have music while we languish here,
Loud music, to annul our spirit's strife,
To make the soul with pleasant fancies rife,
And soothe the stranger from another sphere !

That old-world story of a Saviour's love?
In thy glad loyalties he bears no part ;
He wonders at the rapture in thine eye ;
Negation has no bond with ecstasy !

The whole sonnet (in its original form) is included in Coleridge's approving mark.

[1] '*The Muses, Pagan damsels, with Peter's shadow? Perhaps I do not understand the passage. But the thought which the place seems to me to demand is this. "Haste, Mourner, to the world within thee, haste! There wait thy own spirit, that, like Peter's shadow, will fall and heal thee in his passing."*

'*By the bye*, pass'd *and* haste ! *My old master used on such rhymes to exclaim, "Marble and Tea-spoon, boy !"*'—*S.T.C.*

This sonnet was not republished in any of the later volumes.

XVI.

SUPPOSED TO BE WRITTEN BY ONE ON WHOM THE DEATH OF AN EXCELLENT WOMAN HAS FORCED THE CONVICTION OF A FUTURE STATE.

O'erladen with sad musings, till the tear
Sprang to the pressure, I survey'd thy tomb,
All drest in flowers, as though above thy bier,
Thy breath, yet hovering, fed the gentle bloom ;
I said, 'Maria, though I deem'd too long
That souls would fade like music on the air,
Hast thou not brought me confirmation strong
That they shall yet be beautiful elsewhere ?
For thine was so immaculate and rare,
That but the thought of thy deep purity,
Link'd with that other thought, I could not bear ;
Mount then ! bright soul ! and take thy place on high ;
I do confess thou wert so good and fair
That such as thou were never born to die !' [1]

---

[1] '*It were morose not to approve of these lines. But, alas ! I am too old, weak, and suffering, to have any taste for this filagree religion : or for any other ground of the hope of a resurrection to Life but that which I breathe forth in the prayer, "Almighty Father, of Thy free, unmerited, yea demerited, Love and goodness, have mercy on me, thy poor, infirm, sinful, and most miserable creature, for Christ's sake."*'—S.T.C.

XVII.

(Continued.)

The bliss of Heaven, Maria, shall be thine !
Joy link'd to joy by amaranthine bond !
And a fair harp of many strings divine
Shall meet thy touch with unimagined sound !
Meek angel-hood shall dwell within thine eye,
Fed by the action of thy purer soul ;
Thy brow shall beam with fairer dignity—
No more thy cheek shall blench with Care's control,
Nor yield its hues to changes of the heart,
That beats with plenitude of life and woe—
Taking all dyes that sorrow can impart,
Or ever-shifting circumstance bestow :
The prey of present pangs or after-smart,
For ever feeling pain or missing bliss below.[1]

---

[1] '*I prefer this much to XVI., though both are good.*'—
S.T.C.

The whole of this is marked.

XVIII.

We cannot keep delight—we cannot tell
One tale of steady bliss, unwarp'd, uncrost,
The timid guest anticipates farewell,
And will not stay to hear it from his host !
I saw a child upon a summer's day,
A child upon the margin of a pond,
Catch at the boughs that came within his way,
From a fair fruit-tree on the bank beyond ;
The gale that sway'd them from him aye arose,
And seldom sank into such kindly calm
As gave his hand upon the bunch to close ;
Which then but left its fragrance on his palm ;
For the wind woke anew from its repose,
And bore the fruit away, but wafted all its balm.[1]

---

[1] *'What sort of a fruit-tree could this have been ? orange or lemon ? These have fragrant bunches—and ripe fruit at the same time. But the boughs are sadly unfit for swaying in a breeze.'—S.T.C.*

This sonnet was never republished.

XIX.

A CALM EVENING.

Seest thou how clear and sharp the shadows are
Among the cattle on yon ridgy field,
So softly glooming amid light so fair?
Yon mighty trees no blast may dare to wield ;
The things that own most motion and most sound
Are tranced and silent ; all is mute around.[1]
Where is the wind?   Not in yon glassy sky,
Not in the trees,—what deep tranquillity
Has hush'd his voice?   Methinks so calm should fall
The eve before the great millennial morn,
Before the first of those high days is born,
Whose placid tenor shall be peace to all.
Sink deeply in my heart, surpassing scene ![2]
And be thy memory clear, for I would live therein !

---

[1] The original had 'in a golden swound.' Upon which Coleridge makes the following note :—'*Od's wounds. Such gypsy jargon suits my* "Ancient Mariner," *but surely not this highly classical and polished diction.*'

[2] '*Suffer me, my dear young Poet, to conjure you never to use this Covent Garden and Drury Lane word unless some distinct allusion or reference be made to a Theatre.   This* " *scene and scenery* " (*are*) *villanous slang fineries of the day.*'—*S. T. C.*

XX.

COLLISION OF THE AYR AND COMET STEAMBOATS.

Vessel of Britain ! proudly wert thou going,
Thy strong foundations seated in the sea,
Yet moving like the wind.   The hearts were glowing,
The steps were light, the melody was free,
That usher'd in that midnight jollity ;
Sad was the shock, and fearful was the doom,
That quench'd those happy hearts so suddenly ;
And sad it was to see their kindred come
In quest o' the dearest brow, with hushing breath ;
Oh ! that those blessèd days should ne'er return,
When Christ was ready at the gates of Death
To bid them back, whom widowed souls would mourn !
To make the parents' hope revive and burn,
' Why sorrowest thou ? thy child but slumbereth.' [1]

---

[1] '*I could almost envy young Tennyson the feeling of this sonnet. Alas ! my stern reflection on reading it was—Restore the crew to life ? For what ? A few, perhaps, to be hung, and how many to deserve hanging. But it is constitutional with me, that I cannot, I never could, sympathise with the fear of Death, as Death.*'—*S. T. C.*

XXI.

ON STARTLING SOME PIGEONS.

A hundred wings are dropt as soft as one,
Now ye are lighted !   Pleasing to my sight
The fearful circle of your wondering flight,
Rapid and loud, and drawing homeward soon ;
And then, the sober chiding of your tone,
As there ye sit, from your own roofs arraigning
My trespass on your haunts, so boldly done,
Sounds like a solemn and a just complaining :
O happy, happy race ! for though there clings
A feeble fear about your timid clan,
Yet are ye blest ! with not a thought that brings
Disquietude,—while proud and sorrowing man,
An eagle, weary of his mighty wings,
With anxious inquest fills his little span ! [1]

---

[1] ' *A sweet sonnet, and, with the exception of the one word
" little," faultless.   " Little " may be a proper word, if man
had been here contemplated positively.   He is not so comparatively
in his Eagle-relation to the pigeons.*'—*S. T. C.*

In this sonnet, as republished in 1868, ' little ' is changed
to ' mortal.'

XXII.

Seest thou her blushes, that like shadows sweet
Pass upward from the silence of the heart,
Avowing its fond dream by token meet—
Their crimson traits dissolve, but not depart
The hopes they usher to the lover's breast :
The signature has melted from the bond,
But he doth trust it, asking nought beyond
What promise all so briefly hath imprest ;
Deep in her virgin heart hath sunk the glow—
But thou hast culled its promise, and to thee
If lapse of faith or dark misdoubt should be,
'Twill steal into the blenching face of woe,
Chide back thy pulse to its remitted flow,
And tinge despondent thought and misery.[1]

---

[1] '*I do not understand these four last lines. Perhaps the fault is in myself : but to me they are obscure.*'—*S. T. C.*

In the volume published in 1873 this sonnet was included ; but with so many changes that the shortest way of exhibiting the transformation will be to print the whole.

A BLUSH AT FAREWELL.

Her tears are all thine own ! how blest thou art !
Thine, too, the blush which no reserve can bind ;
Thy farewell voice was as the stirring wind
That floats the rose-bloom ; thou hast won her heart ;
Dear are the hopes it ushers to thy breast ;
She speaks not—but she gives her silent bond ;
And thou may'st trust it, asking nought beyond
The promise, which as yet no words attest ;
Deep in her bosom sinks the conscious glow,
And deep in thine ! and I can well foresee,

XXIII.

A PERVERSE LOVER.

(IPSE LOQUITUR.)

I trust thee from my soul, O Mary dear !
But oft, when Rapture hath its fullest power,
Hope treads too lightly for herself to hear ;
And Doubt is ever by until the hour.
I trust thee, Mary, but till thou art mine
Up from thy foot unto thy golden hair,
Oh ! let me still misgive thee and repine,
Uncommon fears spring up with blessings rare !
Thine eyes of purest love give surest sign,
Drooping with fondness, and thy blushes tell
A flitting tale of steadiest truth and zeal ;
Yet I will doubt, to make success divine !
A tide of summer dreams with gentlest swell
Will bear upon me then, and I shall love most well ! [1]

If thou shalt feel a lover's jealousy
For her brief absence, what a ruling power
A byegone blush shall prove ! until the hour
Of meeting, when thy next love-rose shall blow.

[1] As originally published, this sonnet had no title. The title was added in the reprint in 1873 ; where also the concluding couplet is changed, for

' And when at length I've realised my prize,
Thy husband's heart shall trust thee till it dies.'

XXIV.

ON A PICTURE OF THE FATES.[1]

Ye dull and loathly sisterhood forlorn !
Why did the fabling soul of ancient song
Build up a falsehood of such dreary scorn,
As that to you our being should belong ?
Likening a life that feels so much of heaven,
And so divinely sensible of joy,
To a frail thread at your cold mandate riven,
For hands so pale to weave and to destroy ?
Soul-deadening lore ! that had long since its birth,
When the strange perjury of ancient creed
Jarred in full discord,—now our hearts are freed,
And solemn Reason dictates to the Earth,
Since that most perfect Law shone forth to bless,
That hath no peer in moral loveliness.

---

[1] Arthur Hallam wrote a sonnet on the Fates at the same
time. See *Remains of A. H. H.* p. 32.

*ON THE PICTURE OF THE THREE FATES IN THE
PALAZZO PITTI AT FLORENCE, USUALLY ASCRIBED
TO MICHEL-ANGIOLO.*

None but a Tuscan hand could fix ye here
   In rigidness of sober colouring.
   Pale are ye, mighty Triad, not with fear,
   But the most awful knowledge, that the spring
Is in you of all birth, and act, and sense.
   I sorrow to behold ye : pain is blent
   With your aloof and loveless permanence,
   And your high princedom seems a punishment.

XXV.

MARTIAL ARDOUR IN AGE.

Oh ! if ye marvel that mine eye doth glow
Now every pulse of fervid youth is lost,
Ye never heard the kingly trumpets blow,
Nor felt the fieldward stirring of a host ;
Nor how the bayonet assures the hand
That it can never fail, while Death doth stand
Amid the thunders of the reckless drum,
And the loud scorn of fifes, ashamed and dumb !
Nor, when the noble revel dies away,
How proud they lie upon the stainèd mould,
A presence too majestic to gainsay,
Of lordly martial bearing, mute and cold,
Which Honour knows o' th' instant ! such as lay
On Morat late, or Marathon of old !

The cunning limner could not personate
　Your blind control, save in th' aspect of grief ;
　So doth the thought repugn of sovran Fate.
Let him gaze here, who trusts not in the love
　Toward which all being solemnly doth move.
　More this grand sadness tells, than forms of fairest life.

XXVI.

ON SEEING A CHILD BLUSH ON HIS FIRST
VIEW OF A CORPSE.

'Tis good our earliest sympathies to trace !
And I would muse upon a little thing ;
What brought the blush into that infant's face
When first confronted with the rueful king ?
He boldly came—what made his courage less ?
A signal for the heart to beat less free
Are all imperial presences, and he
Was awed by Death's consummate kingliness ;
A strange bewilder'd look of shame he wore ;
'Twas the first mortal hint that cross'd the lad ;
He fear'd the stranger, though he knew no more,
Surmising and surprised, but, most, afraid,
As Crusoe, wandering on the desert shore,
Saw but an alien footmark and was sad !

XXVII.

TO THE ROBIN.

The ox is all as happy in his stall
As when he low'd i' the summer's yellow eve,
Browsing the king-cup slopes ; but no reprieve
Is left for thee, save thy sweet madrigal,
Poor robin : and severer days will fall.
Bethink thee well of all yon frosted sward,
The orchard-path, so desolate and hard,
And meadow-runnels, with no voice at all !
Then feed with me, poor warbler, household bird,
And glad me with thy song so sadly timed,
And be on thankful ears thy lay conferr'd ;
So, till her latest rhyme my muse hath rhymed,
Thy voice shall with a pleasant thrill be heard.
And with a poet's fear, when twigs are limed.

XXVIII.

THE BUTTERFLY.[1]

Alexis seized a prison'd butterfly
To set it free, on a bright morn of May ;
But the kind touch brush'd half the tints away
From the rich wings, though handled tenderly.
Then spake he out to bashful Isabel,—
'Behold sweet Nature's venturous faith ! and say,
Why thou dost aye refuse thy heart to stay
On mine, that is so fond and loves so well ?
Is beauty trusted to the morning dews ?
And to the butterfly's mischanceful wing ?
To the dissolving cloud in rainbow hues ?
To the frail tenure of an early spring,
In blossoms and in dyes ?   And must I lose
Claim to such trust,—all Nature's underling ? '

---

[1] This is according to the reprint (1868).   The first six lines
stood thus in the original copy :

'The light-set lustre of this insect's mail
Hath bloom'd my gentlest touch.—This first of May
Hath seen me sweep the shallow tints away
From half his pinion, drooping now and pale !
Look hither, coy and timid Isabel,
Fair Lady, look into my eyes, and say,' &c.

XXIX.

DEATH AND ITS ANTIDOTE.

The strongest hearts grow fearful at the name
Of him who gathers up the coil of things ;
Surceasing breath and life that flies, yet clings,
May be a terror, without touch of shame ;
That worms shall revel in the heart of Pride,
And death-damps chill the brows of happy men,
Is truth avow'd and awful !   When, oh ! when,
Shall I, and those I love, our turn abide ? [1]
But stay, my soul ! with fond assurance call
Those hopes into thy landscape, fain to rise,
Even then, when earth was powerless in the thrall
Of hateful rites, and mythologic ties,
But priceless now, beyond the count of gold ;
Not vague, but true, not fearful, but most bold !

---

[1] This is the reading of these four lines as republished
1873.   In the original edition they stood thus :

> That worms should revel in the shrines of pride,
> That death should damp the brows of mighty men,
> Is truth avow'd and dreadful.   When, oh ! when
> Shall I stand helpless in the foaming tide ?

XXX.

O God, impart Thy blessing to my cries,
Tho' I trust deeply, yet I daily err ;
The waters of my heart are oft astir,
An Angel's there ! and yet I cannot rise !
I wish that Christ were here among us still,
Proffering His bosom to His servant's brow,
But oh ! that holy voice comes o'er us now
Like twilight echoes from a distant hill :
No mountain-sermons, and no ruthful gaze !
No voice sweet-toned, and blessing all the time !
No cheerly credence gather'd from His face !
No path thro' hamlets in the eve or prime !
No gentle prayers for all our faded race !
And those whose hearts are half-unstrung with crime.[1]

---

[1] The whole of this sonnet was distinguished in Coleridge's copy by his approving mark. But there seems to have been something in it which did not satisfy the author's feelings in his later life. When he republished it in 1868, he substituted in the second line, 'I trust but faintly' for 'Tho' I trust deeply ; ' in the fifth, 'I would my Lord' for 'I wish that Christ ; ' in the seventh, 'holy life' for 'holy voice ; ' and for the last six, these which follow :

> 'We long for His pure looks and words sublime ;
> His lowly-lofty innocence and grace ;
> The talk sweet-toned, and blessing all the time ;
> The mountain sermon and the ruthful gaze ;
> The cheerly credence gather'd from His face ;
> His voice in village-groups at eve or prime ! '

F

XXXI.

O! it is sweet to weave aërial ties
With fair and fond creations of our own,
To keep the spirit buoyant on the rise
Of that unebbing joyance which alone
Engrosses life,—The consciousness of power
To sluice pure waters from the fount of song,
And far in lordly eminence to tower
Above the world on pinions swift and strong;
Confronting greatness in her every form,
By the deep sea, and where the thunders lower
To pour from out their skirts th' Atlantic storm;
To keep unfading impress of each hour
That Nature's beauty hallows, and to know
Which is the purest tone her voice doth yield below ! [1]

---

[1] This sonnet was not republished in any of the later volumes.

XXXII.

DECADENCE OF GREECE, 1830.

TO ——

Young tourist to the land whose hope has pass'd !
Fain would I seek with thee those shores sublime
That hear no promise from the lips of Time,
Of hours so bright as those he overcast !
There is that Athens ! still in ruin fair,
Though long gone by her intellectual reign ;
Arcadia waits in patient beauty there,
To hear her lingering shepherd's voice again !
Too oft our travellers ply a clumsy art
Here in the West ! No faithful light they lend ;
But keep the dues of Fame so ill apart,
That the great claims of mount and valley blend ;
Misname the passes with incurious ease,
And mix the records of the plashing seas !

XXXIII.

TO ——

Thought travels past thee with intenser glow,
And nobler visions burn upon thine eye,
Than other souls e'er knew of, or can know ;
Massing delicious thought, and fancies high,
From hour to hour, thy spirit teems with joy,
Nor seldom with unrest ; for, when the mind
O'er many themes keeps survey unconfined,
Death will be one ;—'tis surely sad to die !
Placed at the limit of all mortal being,
The mute unquestionable shadow stands,
Whose simple mandate binds the giant's hands
Helpless, and seals the keenest eye from seeing !
We own his power, but know not whence he came ;
We call him Death—he telleth not his name ! [1]

---

[1] In the original edition the last line was the last but one,
and the last but one the last.

XXXIV.

AN ENGLISH CHURCH.

The bells awake the Sabbath's choral prime,
By breezes soften'd to a harp-like tone ;
Lowly and sweetly from the distance thrown,
They greet the ear with jubilee and chime ;
Follow the sound, and it will lead thee on
Into an English church, the home of Prayer,
For who shall say she is not lovelier there,
Than in all other fanes beneath the Sun?
There, if thou doubtest, may it not impart
Fresh hope, to learn that others' hope is sure?
There, duly as the merchant to the mart,
Come aged men, whom daily death makes fewer ;
There all the spirit of a Christian heart
Is bodied forth in gentle rites and pure.

XXXV.

A MOURNING LOVER.

(IPSE LOQUITUR.)

Thou sittest at thy lyre, O lady sweet !
Teaching it all thine own delicious soul ;
Thy voice, the while, swells richly o'er the whole,
And greets mine ear, for Angel-ears more meet ;
Unhappy me ! not for another's bliss,
But that thou art the blessing ! soon to me
Though now thy song doth sound so dear and free,
Its spell shall vanish in another's kiss ;
Unhappy me ! my wounds must ever smart ;
Alas ! for fruitless love !　Alas ! for them,
Who pluck the flowers and press them to their heart,
Though other hands must claim the vital stem,
And all its future bloom ; I know thou art
Powerless to save, though hating to condemn.

XXXVI.

JOY CAME FROM HEAVEN.

Joy came from heaven, for men were mad with pain,
And sought a mansion on this earth below ;
He could not settle on the wrinkled brow,
Close-gather'd to repel him ; and, again,
Upon the cheek he sought repose in vain ;
He found that pillow all too chill and cold,
Where sorrow's streams might float him from his hold,
Caught sleeping in their channel.   Th' eye would fain
Receive the stranger on her slippery sphere,
Where life had purer effluence than elsewhere,
But where no barrier might forbid the tear
To sweep it, when it listed.   So not there
He staid, nor could the lips his couch prepare,
Shifting untenably from smile to sneer.

XXXVII.

SILKWORMS AND SPIDERS.

The worm long fosters his transforming sleep,
But claims the inalienable life again,
Which, tho' it be but one, yet seemeth twain,
The trance between is all so deadly deep ;
The careful spider spreads before his lair
The web he gathers near his filmy heart,
Without the throe of any vital smart,
And of his entrails makes a useful snare :
In both a mighty mystery resides,
A truth, on whose development they thrive ;
One for the cravings of his life provides,
One weaves himself another way to live ;
To search the secret is beyond our lore,
And we must rest, till God shall tell us more.

XXXVIII.

A BIRTHDAY.

The summer tide has brought my natal hour :
Comes it to usher days of bliss or bane?
To set a seal on grief? or to empower
With tenfold strength the tyranny of pain?
Oh ! might we summon back by charm of art,
Those days of bloodless food and placid sleep,
Which crept, exhaling from the mother's heart,
So holy, dreamless, innocent, and deep !
We leave the womb to slumber on the breast,
We leave the breast to climb upon the knee,
Soon beckon'd off by dolour and unrest,
Till our first sympathies are hard to see,
Which passion's heavy overgrowths invest,
Scarce disentwined by keen Philosophy !

XXXIX.

GREECE: AN ASPIRATION.

WRITTEN AT THE TIME OF PRINCE LEOPOLD'S [1] PROPOSED
ELECTION FOR THE THRONE OF GREECE.

Now we may roam along thy flowery dales,
Fair Greece ! and where each ancient fountain flows ;
Now may we pluck at will the lily and rose,
That bloom so sweetly down thy noble vales.
How strange to hear that Attic nightingale
Of old KOLONOS, dear to thee and us !
Or haply catch—if listening may avail
To catch—the lonely voice of Œdipus,
Or wail of choral sorrow from the Past
For wild Medea's wrath. On plain and wold
Thy fanes are free to crumble undefaced,
For Britain's future poets to behold,
That they may keep that sum of memories fast
Which haunts thy ruins from the days of old ! [2]

---

[1] The late King of the Belgians.
[2] This is the reading of this sonnet as republished in 1873.
For the lines beginning 'How strange,' &c., the original edition
had :

> 'And ye are free, Arcadian nightingales,
> To lavish on the air your tuneful woes,
> That sweetly rise and with all sweetness close,
> Where high Lycæus breathes of rural tales
> And Pan, and jealous Lucretil surpast :
> The fanes upon each ruin-covered wold,
> They too are free,' &c.

XL.

THE EARTHQUAKE.

On from the spot, that felt the first dismay,
His mighty path the running Earthquake clove ;
While Ruin, aye attendant on his way,
Sped swiftly o'er the quaking realms above ;
Slowly the seasons do transform the grove,
Most other change is wrought with soft delay,
Save this, which turns the course of streams astray,
Once and for evermore ! when to remove
The landmarks of this earth our Maker wills,
The work is done with noises harsh and loud,
And lightning speed ; such ministry fulfils
The 'hest of Him by whom the heavens are bow'd ;
Whose throne is compass'd with a mystic cloud,
Who touches into smoke th' eternal hills.[1]

---

[1] This and the three next sonnets are printed from the 1873 edition. The original has been a good deal corrected in all of them, but only by way of improvement in point of composition. In the first edition, the last two lines stood thus :

When he descendeth down on Zion hill,
While darkness is beneath him, like a cloud.

XLI.

THE 'CANNON FEVER.'

The tide of things should flow less troubled, sure ;
To clear its current sages do impart
Their wisdom, and the poet's pitying heart
Pours in its crystal tribute, bright and pure ;
But still doth War present a mighty lure
To many minds ; a charm which lulls to rest
Compunctious thought, and mails the obdurate breast
With triple-plated iron, to endure
The shock of children's cries and woman's tears,
Untouch'd, unsoften'd, and without a sigh ;
O Glory without Honour !   Helms and spears
School to a ruthless calm the warrior's eye ;
'Carnage' he means, when he cries 'Victory,'[1]
And barren battle hath his hopes and fears !

---

[1] 'Licence they mean when they cry Liberty.'
                                        MILTON.

XLII.

THE PRISONER.

His was a chamber in the topmost tower—
A small unsightly cell with grated bars ;
And wearily went on each irksome hour
Of dim captivity and moody cares ;
Against such visitants he was not strong,
But sat with laden heart and brow of woe ;
And every morn he heard the stir and song
Of birds in royal gardens far below,
Telling of bowers and dewy lawns unseen,
Drench'd with the silver steam that night had shed ;
Part blossom-white, part exquisitely green,
By little warblers roam'd and tenanted,
Blending their glad wild notes to greet the sheen
Of the May Dawn, that gleam'd upon his bed.[1]

---

[1] The whole of this sonnet was marked in Coleridge's copy,
as one that he particularly liked. In that copy the last five
lines stood thus :

> Drench'd with the silver steam that night had left—
> Part blossom-white, part exquisitely green,
> And ringing all with thrushes on the left,
> And finches on the right, to greet the sheen
> Of the May-dawn ; while he was thus bereft !

XLIII.

THE PORTRAIT PAINTER.

No feeble glow of intellectual flame
Inform'd that Painter's heart ; to none more due
Than him, the honours of domestic fame ;
What hand, but his, so excellently knew
The shadow of our lineaments ? In vain
The glance of Beauty dared his subtle skill,
Touch'd into all its sympathies again,
Kindled anew with all its power to kill ;
Age smiled, portray'd in all its sober calm,
Unvext, of grandsire aspect, pale and meek ;
And babyhood, with hands too small for harm ;
And youth, with full and health-ensanguined cheek,
Show'd life-like on his chart, and boyhood sleek
Still wore his dimpled chin, and merry charm.

XLIV.

SUPPOSED TO BE WRITTEN BY ANY FEEBLE-MINDED MAN MEDITATING SELF-DESTRUCTION.

Sweet brother-soul ! I may not tarry here ;
The grave is made for me—if joy had been
But rarely visitant or dimly seen,
I would not thus have call'd the distance near,
Or summon'd for my peace this early bier :
But happiness long-while hath kept aloof,
An alien to my heart, which was not proof
Against the lacking of a thing so dear :
The hour is drawing nigh, when this wild heart
Shall be the thrall of worms, and know it not,
As calm as peace can be. No pulse or start
Of reviviscence, till the life hath got
Its flow again, which had but ebb'd in part :
But never more to feel the sinner's earthly lot ! [1]

---

[1] The first eleven lines of this sonnet, down to 'As calm as peace can be' are marked in Coleridge's copy. But it was not republished in any later volume.

XLV.

TO A. H. H.

When youth is passing from my hoary head,
And life's decline steals brightness from thine eye—
But *that* it cannot soon, nor quench the red
Upon thy cheek that hath so rich a dye—
Then of what crowns of fame may thou and I
Avow ourselves the gainers? with what balm
Of Christian hope, devotionally calm,
Shall I be then anointed? Will this sigh,
Born of distemper'd feeling, still come forth
As thus, unjoyous? or be left to die
Before the rapid and unpausing birth
Of joyous thoughts succeeding momently?
What would not such recoil of bliss be worth,
Replacing in our age this early loss of joy?[1]

---

[1] This was never republished.

XLVI.

A FOREST LAKE.

O lake of sylvan shore ! when gentle Spring
Slopes down upon thee from the mountain side,
When birds begin to build and brood and sing ;
Or, in maturer season, when the pied
And fragrant turf is throng'd with blossoms rare ;
In the frore sweetness of the breathing morn,
When the loud echoes of the herdsman's horn
Do sally forth upon the silent air
Of thy thick forestry, may I be there,
While the wood waits to see its phantom born
At clearing twilight, in thy glassy breast ;
Or, when cool eve is busy, on thy shores,
With trails of purple shadow from the West,
Or dusking in the wake of tardy oars.[1]

---

[1] The whole of this sonnet is marked in Coleridge's copy ;
which differed from this only in having 'the loud pealing of the
huntsman's horn' in the seventh line, instead of 'the loud
echoes of the herdsman's horn.'

XLVII.

TO ——

A lovely vision fading out of sight,
Pure waters fast a-draining, these may be
Apt semblance of a truth well-known to thee,
Poor pallid maid ! thou canst not reunite
Nor blend again the colours of thy heart—
The secret nurture of a healthy mind
Will long preserve, perchance may half impart,
The cheek's pure glow, to sorrow ne'er assign'd ;
But thine is cold and pale, as might beseem
A rose-bud planted in a vase of snow,
Which droops full soon, as it did surely know
Of the thin flakes collapsing round its stem ;
Even thus thy cheek has lost its vital glow,
Because there is no source of kindly warmth below ! [1]

---

[1] In this the four lines beginning 'But thine is cold,' &c.
have Coleridge's approving mark. But the sonnet was not
republished.

XLVIII.

THE RAINBOW.

Hung on the shower that fronts the golden West,
The Rainbow bursts like magic on mine eyes !
In hues of ancient promise there imprest ;
Frail in its date, eternal in its guise ;
The vision is so lovely, that I feel
My heart imbued with beauty like its own,
And taking an indissoluble seal
From what is here a moment, and is gone ;
It lies so soft on the full-breasted storm,
New-born o' the middle air, and dewy-pure,
And trick'd in Nature's choicest garniture ;
What can be seen of lovelier dye or form ?
While all the groves assume a ghastly stain,
Caught from the leaden rack and shining rain ! [1]

---

[1] In this the three lines beginning 'It lies so soft,' &c. are marked in Coleridge's copy.

XLIX.

ON A GENIUS OF LOWLY ESTATE.

Where may not souls be found to greatness true?
Born with no loftier hope or prouder aim
Than lineage lowly, like his own, could claim,
How did he guess at his immortal due?
How was the fire first smitten from the steel?
When came that strange enforcement of his will?
How did his mind, 'mid poverty and ill,
Find leisure to endow itself so well?
Methinks, one summer's eve, he first did hear
The rise and fall of music in his heart;
Wild notes, a-dropping downward without art
To a sweet close, that fell upon his ear
Unutterably soft, and yet most clear,
And seeming from his bosom's depth to start.[1]

---

[1] In this Coleridge's approving mark includes the whole.

*The following Sonnets, as far as No. CXLVIII.,
were published in* 1864 *and dedicated to Alfred Tenny-
son.*

L.

PREFATORY.

I dream'd I wrote an ode, and was not slack
To bring it where two mighty umpires dealt
The prize ; but deep-mouth'd Pindar bade me back,
And laughing Horace—like a boy I felt,
Who, idly thrumming on a single hair,
Stretch'd from his forehead, with his simple head
And child's ear close upon it, fancy-fed,
Conceits himself a harpist then and there ;
I woke, and murmur'd o'er a humbler strain,
A sonnet—smiling at my classic dream—
But still I may misuse some honest theme,
Tinkling this idle outgrowth of my brain ;
A hair amid the harpstrings ! my weak words
May pass unheard among the rolling chords.

LI.

GREAT LOCALITIES. AN ASPIRATION.

Oft do I muse in castle-building hours—
O ! might some trick o' the air advance the hill
Of Sion westward, I would gaze my fill
Upon her far-projected walls and towers !
O ! that the realms our rounded earth doth hide
Could, maugre all the horizons, be display'd
To my rapt eyes and heart—o'er land and tide
By some intense refractive power convey'd !
For I am bound by duties and constraints
To mine own land, or move in modest round
Among my neighbours ; tho' my spirit faints
And hungers for the storied eastern ground :
Cease, dreamer ! is it fit the laws of space
And vision should be strain'd to meet thy case ?

LII

Continued.

But, if it were, how soon Jerusalem
Should front my homestead with her mountain-hold !
And ever-listening hills of Bethlehem
Report themselves in colours clear and bold !
Then would I summon here old Cheops' tomb,
With its broad base to flank my bordering wood——
A mighty phantom ! pressing for the room
It holds in Egypt ! next, with change of mood,
Fair Athens should be welcomed, and the rest
Of those immortal cities, one by one ;
And, for my latest atmospheric guest,
I'd bid that crumbled mound from Babylon
Come looming up at sundown, with the moan
Of evening winds, and shadows from the west.

LIII.

Continued.

Nor—could I bring within my visual scope
The great localities old stories boast—
Would I forget thee, Troas ! whose first hope
Of travel pointed to thy lonely coast ;
How would my quicken'd fancy reproduce
Th' incessant brazen flash of Homer's war,
And heroes moving quick their ground to choose,
With spear-tops burning like the autumn star,
Along that sullen sea-board ! till, at length,
Mine ear should thrill, my startled pulses bound,
When from the trench those two grand voices rose—
And each involved in th' other, swept their foes
Before them, like a storm—the wrath and strength
Of God and man conspiring to the sound !

LIV.

TOKEN LIGHTS. A CONTRAST.

Of old, when Greek and Trojan took the field,
Before a lance was thrown or goat-horn bended,
The god, who on some favourite chief attended
Lit up a sudden flame from helm and shield ;
We need no palpable approach of fire,
No visual intimation to be made,
Nor do we with our natural eyes require
To test our Guardian-God's protecting aid ;
From holier heavens our token-lights descend
Upon our Christian weapons, zeal and love,
To embolden and support us to the end
Of that great war thro' which we daily move,
To raise our drooping hearts and give us sight
Of our great Master's presence in the fight.

LV.

GREAT LOCALITIES. ROME.

Keen was the vision which Ambition lent
To Rome's great captains, when the vacant realm
Was waiting for a chief to seize the helm,
And their stern martial looks were southward bent
From Gaul or Britain, like a wizard's gaze
Constraining some weak victim to his harm,
While yet the nations had no countercharm
Against a despot's eye, in those fierce days ;
The city of their greed seem'd well-nigh theirs,
Half in their grasp, full clearly bodied forth ;
My Rome should softly float into the north
At my fond wish, convoy'd by gentle airs--
Rapt into Freedom's land a little while
From Pio's grief, and Antonelli's guile !

LVI.

THE MOSELLE BOATMAN AND HIS DAUGHTER.

Not high nor full enough to show things clear,
The half moon hung above the mountain-lines—
But, glancing on the waters, kindled there
A lamp of gold beneath the unseen vines ;
The night was fair, but, as our port we near'd,
We sigh'd to lose the boatman and his mate,
Between whose patient faces we had sate,
The old man rowing, while his daughter steer'd ;
' Father,' she oft would say in accents mild,
Whene'er she asked advice, or craved reply
To some brief question, while, with loving eye,
He smiled and nodded to his wistful child,
Over his close-join'd hands and labouring oar—
'Twas sad to think we ne'er might see them more !

LVII.

Continued.

When first we took the stream, the maiden held
The oar, to keep her father's strength unworn
For midday labour ; but the sight compell'd
Our pity, and the aid of pity born—
For at each stroke, whose ripples reach'd the land,
She rose up bodily, with toil and pain,
And often paused, and dipp'd her little hand,
To cool her brow, yet did she not complain ;
Full oft, in day-dreams of that sweet Moselle,
I seek my gentle Gretchen, and persuade
My questing memory that all goes well
At Alf, by Bertrich, with that village-maid,
Who, when the task her slender force outweigh'd,
Rose from her seat, to make her rowing tell.

LVIII.

THE BLUSH OF CONSTANTINE AT THE COUNCIL OF NICE.

To that high Council gather'd to compose
The troubled waters of the Church of Christ,
And with her noble words convince her foes,
Came the great monarch, faithful to his tryst ;
But lo ! on entering, how his visage glows
With sudden reverence, that doth enlist
The sympathies of bishop, courtier, priest ;
Who gaze in tender silence on the rose
He brings to their first meeting, and address
Themselves with braver hearts to their grand cause ;
And, though in aftertimes his zeal grew less
For the pure creed of those whose eyes he draws,
All is congenial now.   They find no flaw
In that king's-aspect, dash'd with holy awe.

LIX.

CONSTANTINE'S AMPHITHEATRE AT TRÈVES.

This is the spot, where mighty Constantine,
His pagan pride o'ermatching Christian thought,
With his fair baths and palace did conjoin
The vast arena where his captives fought :
Strange ! that the first great prince who stood for God,
Should disaffect his new-won creed so far,
As thus to dally with the lust of blood,
And feed himself in peace with shows of war !
Here, where the crowd, 'mid plaudits and alarms,
With brief stern action seal'd the will of Rome,
The vines outstretch their ever-floating arms,
That mark no victim, and denounce no doom ;
But round the ancient circuit waving stand,
To swell the vintage of this peaceful land.

LX.

THE LION'S SKELETON.

How long, O lion, hast thou fleshless lain?
What rapt thy fierce and thirsty eyes away?
First came the vulture : worms, heat, wind, and rain
Ensued, and ardors of the tropic day.
I know not—if they spared it thee—how long
The canker sate within thy monstrous mane,
Till it fell piecemeal, and bestrew'd the plain ;
Or, shredded by the storming sands, was flung
Again to earth ; but now thine ample front,
Whereon the great frowns gather'd, is laid bare ;
The thunders of thy throat, which erst were wont
To scare the desert, are no longer there ;
Thy claws remain, but worms, wind, rain, and heat
Have sifted out the substance of thy feet.

LXI.

THE ARROW-KING.

How shall I picture forth the eagle's flight?
An arrow feather'd with two mighty vans,
That soars and stoops at will, and broadly scans
The woods and waters with a living sight!
A wondrous arrow! wheeling round and round,
Before its prone descent upon the prey,
Descried far off upon the subject ground,
And with one stroke disabled for the fray;
But lo! there comes a small, unpennon'd thing,
And, from the rifle's throat directly sped,
Is potent to bring down this arrow-king,
With slacken'd wing and self-abandon'd head.
His nearest foe is yonder human eye,
With no assailant else in earth or sky!

LXII.

CYNOTAPHIUM.

When some dear human friend to death doth bow,
Fair blooming flowers are strewn upon the bier,
And haply, in the silent house, we hear
The last wild kiss ring on the marble brow,
And lips that never miss'd reply till now ;
And thou, poor dog, wert in thy measure dear—
And so I owe thee honour, and the tear
Of friendship, and would all thy worth allow.
In a false world, thy heart was brave and sound ;
So, when my spade carved out thy latest lair,
A spot to rest thee on, I sought and found—
It was a tuft of primrose, fresh and fair,
And, as it was thy last hour above ground,
I laid thy sightless head full gently there.

H

LXIII.

Continued.

' I cannot think thine all is buried here,'
I said, and sigh'd—the wind awoke and blew
The morning-beam along the gossamer,
That floated o'er thy grave all wet with dew ;
A hint of better things, however slight,
Will feed a loving hope ; it soothed my woe
To watch that little shaft of heavenly light
Pass o'er thee, moving softly to and fro :
Within our Father's heart the secret lies
Of this dim world ; why should *we only* live
And what was I that I should close mine eyes
On all those rich presumptions, that reprieve
The meanest life from dust and ashes ?   Lo !
How much on such dark ground a gleaming thread
        can do !

LXIV.

THE VACANT CAGE.

Our little bird in his full day of health
With his gold-coated beauty made us glad,
But when disease approach'd with cruel stealth,
A sadder interest our smiles forbad.
How oft we watch'd him, when the night hours came,
His poor head buried near his bursting heart,
Which beat within a puft and troubled frame ;
But he has gone at last, and play'd his part :
The seed-glass, slighted by his sickening taste,
The little moulted feathers, saffron-tipt,
The fountain, where his fever'd bill was dipt,
The perches, which his failing feet embraced,
All these remain—not even his bath removed—
But where's the spray and flutter that we loved ?

LXV.

Continued.

He shall not be cast out like wild-wood things !
We will not spurn those delicate remains ;
No heat shall blanch his plumes, nor soaking rains
Shall wash the saffron from his little wings ;
Nor shall he be inearth'd—but in his cage
Stand, with his innocent beauty unimpair'd ;
And all the skilled'st hand can do, to assuage
Poor Dora's grief, by more than Dora shared,
Shall here be done.   What though these orbs of glass
Will feebly represent his merry look
Of recognition, when he saw her pass,
Or from her palm the melting cherry took—
Yet the artist's kindly craft shall not retain
The filming eye, and beak that gasp'd with pain.

LXVI.

BIRD-NESTING.

Ah ! that half bashful and half eager face !
Among the trees thy guardian angel stands,
With his heart beating, lest thy little hands
Should come among the shadows and efface
The stainless beauty of a life of love,
And childhood innocence—for hark, the boys
Are peering through the hedgerows and the grove,
And ply their cruel sport with mirth and noise ;
But thou hast conquer'd ! and dispell'd his fear ;
Sweet is the hope thy youthful pity brings—
And oft, methinks, if thou shalt shelter here
When these blue eggs are linnets' throats and wings,
A secret spell shall bring about the tree
The little birds that owed their life to thee.

LXVII.

THE LACHRYMATORY.

From out the grave of one whose budding years
Were cropt by death, when Rome was in her prime,
I brought the phial of his kinsman's tears,
There placed, as was the wont of ancient time ;
Round me, that night, in meads of asphodel,
The souls of the early dead did come and go,
Drawn by that flask of grief, as by a spell,
That long-imprison'd shower of human woe ;
As round Ulysses, for the draught of blood,
The heroes throng'd, those spirits flock'd to me,
Where, lonely, with that charm of tears, I stood ;
Two, most of all, my dreaming eyes did see ;
The young Marcellus, young, but great and good,
And Tully's daughter, mourn'd so tenderly.

LXVIII

AN INCIDENT IN A CHURCH.

As one whose eyes, by gleam of waters caught,
Should find them strewn with pansies, so to me
It chanced that morning, as I bow'd the knee,
Soliciting th' approach of hallow'd thought ;
I dream'd not that so dear a tomb was nigh ;
My sidelong glance the lucid marble drew,
And, turning round about enquiringly,
I found it letter'd with the names I knew ;
Three precious names I knew, and loved withal,
Yea, knew and loved, albeit too briefly known—
Louisa, Henry, and the boy just grown
To boyhood's prime, as each received the call ;
And, over all, carved in the same white stone,
The symbol of the holiest death of all.

LXIX.

Continued.

TO THE SURVIVORS.

Henceforth to you this monument shall be
A bright and constant presence : evermore
Your thoughts of death must pass by this white door,
Till ye yourselves shall meet Eternity ;
This vestal tablet written o'er with love,
From morn to eve your inner eye shall read,
And even in midnight darkness ye shall prove
What heavenward hopes its snowy gleam can feed ;
Yes, ever in your hearts' clear depths shall lie
This fair tomb-shadow, when no ripple moves ;
And, when fresh roused to earthly sympathy,
Come floating softly o'er your living loves :
While I, not robbing you, may keep my share
Of that pure light which stole across my prayer.

LXX.

ON THE DEATH OF TWO LITTLE CHILDREN.[1]

Ah ! bitter chance ! no hand the blow could ward !
Nor shield from harm her little guileless breast,
New to this perilous world, and daily prest
To a fond mother's heart ; her lot seems hard ;
But lo ! her face is calm—a gentle tone
Seems murmuring from those lips that breathe no more,
' Come, little sister, mark'd for heaven before !
I crave that hand, yet smaller than mine own,
That baby-hand, to clasp again in mine !'
Sweet spirit ! as thou wishest, it shall be ;
Death drops his wing on younger heads than thine,
Though thine is of the youngest ; soon to thee
The little sister of thy soul shall come
And one low funeral bell shall bring ye home !

---

[1] Daughters of the Hon. Gustavus and Lady Katharine
Hamilton Russell, the elder of whom died by an accident
during the mortal illness of her sister, who almost immediately
followed her. They were both buried on the same day.

LXXI.

GODDARD AND LYCIDAS.

Two dirges by two poets have I read,
By two great masters of our English tongue ;
One for the youth who rests his drownèd head
Upon the mighty harp of him who sung
The loss of Eden ; and the other, warm
From Wordsworth's gentle heart,[1] o'er Goddard's grave,
By Keller raised, near Zurich's stormy wave—
Both beautiful, with each its proper charm ;
The one so glorious—we are fain to blend
The name of Lycidas with that wild sea,
Where sank to deathless fame the poet's friend :
The other, with a humbler purpose penn'd,
Set one poor mother's stifled sorrows free,
And gain'd, by lowlier means, a sweeter end.

---

[1] ' The first human consolation that the afflicted mother felt
was derived from this tribute to her son's memory ; a fact which
the author learned at his own residence from her daughter who
visited Europe some years afterwards.'—From a note by
Wordsworth to his *Elegiac Stanzas* on Frederick William
Goddard, who was drowned in the Lake of Zurich.

LXXII.

HOPE BENEATH THE WATERS.

' I cannot mount to heaven beneath this ban ;
Can Christian hope survive so far below
The level of the happiness of man ?
Can angels' wings in these dark waters grow ?
A spirit voice replied, ' From bearing right
Our sorest burthens, comes fresh strength to bear ;
And so we rise again towards the light,
And quit the sunless depths for upper air :
Meek patience is as diver's breath to all
Who sink in sorrow's sea, and many a ray
Comes gleaming downward from the source of day,
To guide us reascending from our fall ;
The rocks have bruised thee sore, but angels' wings
Grow best from bruises, hope from anguish springs.'

LXXIII.

THE BUOY-BELL.

How like the leper, with his own sad cry
Enforcing his own solitude, it tolls !
That lonely bell set in the rushing shoals,
To warn us from the place of jeopardy !
O friend of man ! sore-vext by ocean's power,
The changing tides wash o'er thee day by day ;
Thy trembling mouth is fill'd with bitter spray,
Yet still thou ringest on from hour to hour ;
High is thy mission, though thy lot is wild—
To be in danger's realm a guardian sound ;
In seamen's dreams a pleasant part to bear,
And earn their blessing as the year goes round ;
And strike the key-note of each grateful prayer,
Breathed in their distant homes by wife or child !

LXXIV.

THE RAINBOW.

Father of all !   Thou dost not hide Thy bond
As one that would disclaim it—on the cloud,
Or springing fount, or torrent's misty shroud,
Lord of the waters ! are thy tokens found ;
Thy promise lives about the ambient air,
And, ever ready at a moment's call,
Reports itself, in colours fresh and fair ;
And, where St. Lawrence rushes to his fall
In thunder, Thou dost tend his angry breath
Infusing it with rainbows :—one and all
The floods of this green earth attest Thy faith,
The rain, the fountain, and the watery wall—
And, badged with sweet remembrancers, they say,
'My word, once given, shall never pass away.'

LXXV.

ANASTASIS.

Tho' death met love upon thy dying smile,
And staid him there for hours, yet the orbs of sight
So speedily resign'd their aspect bright,
That Christian hope fell earthward for awhile,
Appall'd by dissolution ; but on high
A record lives of thine identity !
Thou shalt not lose one charm of lip or eye ;
The hues and liquid lights shall wait for thee,
And the fair tissues, wheresoe'er they be !
Daughter of heaven ! our grieving hearts repose
On the dear thought that we once more shall see
Thy beauty—like Himself our Master rose—
So shall that beauty its old rights maintain,
And thy sweet spirit own those eyes again.

LXXVI.

THE DEATH-SMILE OF COWPER.

'O orphan smile ! born since our mourner died——
We ever long'd for thee, but saw thee not,
Till now, in posthumous beauty ; nought beside
Could have so moved us, while our tears were hot
And thrilling.   Art thou not to each sad friend
The symbol of a long-desired release?
A lovely prelude of immortal peace,
Now that the storm of life has reach'd its end?'
Fresh from kind Hayley's page these words I wrote,
As though I lean'd o'er Cowper, and beheld,
As present fact, what I from records quote ;
By rapture of pure sympathy impell'd
To join those first eye-witnesses, and note
A death-smile, and the sorrow that it quell'd.

LXXVII.

APPREHENSION OF BLINDNESS.

When first upon mine eyes the darkness came,
I said, ' Will this dull film be always here,
To chide mine eyes with a perpetual fear ?
Or will the blind man's lot my spirit tame ? '
Ah ! thankless heart, and words which bring me shame
To think of ; for a better time was near,
And wiser thoughts, which daily grow more dear,
With deep remorse for that unholy blame :
This web that falls and rises—Heaven be praised !
Thro' its dark meshes I can read Thy Word :
Dim holy hopes have dawn'd where sunshine blazed
Unheeded ; O sweet twilight undeplored !
O floating veil ! full gently dropt and raised
By the good hand of Jesus Christ my Lord.

LXXVIII.

LOSS AND RESTORATION OF SMELL.

Dull to the year's first odours, I rebell'd
Against the law which doom'd the violets
Ere I had smelt them ; but, ere long, I held
A quicken'd nostril over all the sweets
Of the full summer—for I had besought
The All-Giver to restore my blunted sense ;
Humbly I pray'd, and breath of roses brought
The answer.   O ! it was a joy intense,
After that dreary interval of loss.
I laugh'd, I ran about as one possess'd ;
And now that winter seems my hopes to cross
I snuff the very frost with happy zest,
Proud of recover'd power, and fain to win
Fresh triumphs for it, when the Spring comes in.

I

LXXIX.

ON THE STATUE OF LORD BYRON,

By Thorwaldsen, in Trinity College Library, Cambridge.

'Tis strange that I, who haply might have met
Thy living self—who sought to hide the flaws
In thy great fame, and, though I ne'er had set
Eyes on thee, heard thee singing without pause,
And long'd to see thee, should, alas ! detect
The Thyrza-sorrow first on sculptured brows,
And know thee best in marble !   Fate allows
But this poor intercourse ; high and erect
Thou hold'st thy head, whose forward glance beholds
All forms that throng this learned vestibule ;
Women and men, and boys and girls from school,
Who gaze with admiration all uncheck'd
On thy proud lips, and garment's moveless folds,
So still, so calm, so purely beautiful !

LXXX.

Continued.

And near thee hangs a page, in boyhood penn'd,
When all thy thoughts were, like thy marble, pure ;
When thou hadst none but little faults to mend,
In Lochnagar's cool shadow still secure
From praise or slander ; but thy brilliant youth
And manhood soon took tribute of thy kind ;
Great artists then thy lineaments design'd, ·
And, last, the Dane's fine chisel struck the truth ;
And, when the current of the breath of fame
Drew up all relics of the master's craft,
This little page,—we know not whence it came,—
Ran flitting forward in the mighty draught,
And, placed at last, where it was fain to be,
Shares our fond gaze between itself and thee.

I 2

LXXXI.

MARY QUEEN OF SCOTS,

According to her Advocates.

Thou pleadest well, yet some will say, and weep
To say it : 'See, the fond historian stands
Chafing the blood from Mary's snowy hands
In vain, for still their ancient stains they keep ;'
I join them not—I, too, am fain to think
That thou hast wrought a credible disproof
Of that old verdict.   Shall I hold aloof,
And shut my heart up from the veriest blink
Of charitable sunshine, that descends
On this still-closing, still-re-opening bud
Of unproved innocence ?   O Holyrood !
Speak, for thou knowest !   Tell the means, the ends
Of that dark conclave !   All good spirits move
The lost truth to the light ; it is a work of love !

LXXXII.

Continued.

When the young hand of Darnley lock'd in her's
Had knit her to her northern doom—amid
The spousal pomp of flags and trumpeters,
Her fate look'd forth and was no longer hid ;
A jealous brain beneath a southern crown
Wrought spells upon her ; from afar she felt
The waxen image of her fortunes melt
Beneath the Tudor's eye, while the grim frown
Of her own lords o'ermaster'd her sweet smiles—
And nipt her growing gladness, till she mourn'd,
And sank, at last, beneath their cruel wiles ;
But, ever since, all generous hearts have burn'd
To clear her fame, yea, véry babes have yearn'd
Over this saddest story of the isles.

LXXXIII.

QUEEN ELIZABETH.

Yet our Elizabeth stood out alone,
Shielding the faith—though tarnish'd thus with crime,
When any darkness fell upon the time,
She heard the Jesuit's foot steal near the throne ;
When man and nature felt the advancing stress
Of that great armament, her mighty soul
Quail'd not, and England from her steadfastness
Took heart—right-royal was her self-control ;
Thames held his state ; bold headlands of the coast
Sent winds to chafe the foe, that, hinting wreck,
Puft at each tilting prow and tower'd deck,
Till fuller tempests squander'd all their host,
And, like a pack that overruns the scent,
Far to the north their scurrying vessels went !

LXXXIV.

THE ORDER OF THE STAR OF INDIA.

'The star of India !' 'tis a goodly name—
Due to a fuller honour, purer love,
Than we, defaulters to our trust, can claim :
Yet sure its choice was prompted from above ;
Part-offspring of our civil hopes and fears,
Perchance its *style* is loftier than its *birth* ;
But seen by wistful eyes thro' holy tears,
It lengthens out its beam and lights the earth ;
We hail it as the herald of the day,
Earth's noblest badge, and knighthood's brightest prize;
The spirit of Havelock, the pure and wise,
Leans forward to salute it on its way—
And sainted Heber, with a glad surprise
Sees from Almorah's hill its rising ray.

LXXXV.

Continued.

I dream'd—methought I stood upon a strand
Unblest with day for ages ; and despair
Had seized me, but for cooling airs that fann'd
My forehead, and a voice that said ' Prepare !'
Anon I felt a dawning was at hand ;
A planet rose, whose light no cloud could mar,
And made thro' all the landscape near and far,
A wild half-morning for that dreary land ;
I saw her seas come washing to the shore
In sheets of gleaming ripples, wide and fair ;
I saw her goodly rivers brimming o'er,
And from their fruitful shallows look'd the star ;
And all seem'd kiss'd with star-light ! till the beam
Of sunrise broke and yet fulfill'd my dream.

LXXXVI.

A THOUGHT FOR MARCH 1860.

Yon happy blackbird's note the rushing wind
Quells not, nor disconcerts his golden tongue,
That breaks my morning dream with well-known song ;
How many a roaring March I've left behind,
Whose blasts, all-spirited with notes and trills,
Blew over peaceful England ! and, ere long,
Another March will come these hills among,
To clash the lattices and whirl the mills :
But what shall be ere then ?   Ambition's lust
Is broad awake, and gazing from a throne
But newly set, counts half the world his own ;
All ancient covenants aside are thrust,
Old landmarks are like scratches in the dust,
His eagles wave their wings, and they are gone.

LXXXVII.

AUTOCRATIC POLICY OF THE FEDERAL AMERICANS.

At length a fierce autocracy is seen
Install'd aloft in Freedom's very seat ;
A throne built on the anger of defeat—
A virtual crown accorded in a spleen ;
The North, which brawl'd for Freedom and her rights :
The North, which talk'd so big of brotherhood,
Hath dared for very rage a hundred fights,
When once her will was traversed ! Once withstood,
She open'd condor's wings, and cried for blood :
And soar'd at once to sheer despotic heights—
And so we see, O saddest of all sights !
A ravening temper, deaf to all things good ;
While the poor slaves, cajoled by warring whites,
Drift between North and South like floating wood.

LXXXVIII.

POSSIBLE RESULTS OF THE FRIENDS' MISSION TO ST. PETERSBURG.

In the Message of Alexander II. to Congress at the beginning of the war.

Whatever be the meaning of that creed
Of the poke-bonnet and the ample brim,
Still in the shoes of truth the Quakers tread,
When they denounce our wars : forget the prim
Staid aspect of these worthy gentlemen,
While purely, honestly, for peace they plead ;
Nor think it shame to propagate the seed
Sown by the sober hands of William Penn ;
Perchance—when to that Northern court they went,
They left some saddening thoughts of death and war ;
And can we think their words were idly spent,
If that sweet message of the younger Czar
To deaf Americans, were meant to endorse,
By the son's act, the father's late remorse ?

LXXXIX.

Continued.

Prove his own love of peace and sanction theirs,
The very quaintness of that precedent,
Which sought to baulk a warrior-king's intent
By quiet looks, and unofficial prayers,—
Blended with somewhat chivalrous and bold,
Even in the very act of their appeal
To him, full autocrat from head to heel,
Sworn to his own great plans, a lifetime old—
Might hit his fancy with a pleasant zest,
Might haunt his memory with a dim control,
Among a thousand thoughts the last and best,
While that stern leaguer of Sebastopol
Alternately exalted, and deprest,
Day after day, the balance of his soul.

XC.

THE GREAT EXHIBITION OF 1862.

The great Exchanges press each other's heels,
Like the swift seasons or the swifter moons,
All Europe through—and every nation feels
This kindly intercourse the best of boons ;
The paths of peace and commerce, from all sides,
Lie straight for England, like old Roman ways ;
Hither the railway brawls, the steamboat glides,
The desert-ship is steer'd, the sledge-dog bays !
Brought to the coast, and then disburthen'd there,
The o'erladen camel's spongy foot springs home
To its old span, while with a witless stare
He eyes the sea-board and the barks that come
To float his burthen off to the world's Fair :
The dog returns in snowy wilds to roam.

XCI

Continued.

They snuff the breath of intervening seas,
And know no more of London, but the man
Ardent, competitive, and large of plan,
Brings all his spirit to such marts as these
The porterage of sea and land is claim d,
All common means we mend and multiply
Let not these bold preparatives be shamed,
These energies of hope advance to die !
O Art and Commerce, set the nations free,
And bid the rites of war's proud temples cease
O power of steam ! for ever may'st thou be
A rolling incense in the house of peace !
And all these vast consignments but increase
Our sense of brotherhood and charity !

XCII.

HEBRON.

The Prince of Wales's Visit.

Long had the Saracen with ruthless arms,
Denied all access to this place of awe ;
Next came the Christian Church, with holy psalms
Charming the gloom of hollow Machpelah :
Anon, the votaries of Mohammed's name,
Returning, trod the desecrated floors,
And, in the gusts through those re-opening doors,
The dreary Moslem voices went and came
In Jacob's ears !   But now a step draws nigh,
A sound to reassure the patriarch's heart
With promise of the coming time, and start
The cerements from the hollow of his thigh,
As tho' the angel call'd : for lo ! they meet—
The ' Ladder ' and the ' Cross,' with promise sweet !

XCIII.

Continued.

How doth the Crescent brook this mighty change?
Sharpening those idle horns she cannot fill,
She peers with keen regret on that old range
Of tombs, and marks them for seclusion still ;
But Niphon and Cathay are enter'd now
On their new course, and shall the Turk's proud will
Reclose our unseal'd Hebron? and avow
Their stern monopoly of El Khalil?
Help ! England, lend the shelter of thy love—
And let the firm stress of thy brooding wing
Be felt by those bold hands that would remove*
Thy fond protective strength, which soon shall bring
These graves within the scope of Christian eyes,
And let poor Israel share the new-won prize.

XCIV.

Continued.

And when the coveted blessing is once gain'd,
And Israel to his father's tomb shall come,
By Christian aid recover'd and maintain'd,
Oh may his heart for Christian hope find room !
And, as he leans and listens, inly thrill'd,
May that dark chasm give forth One mystic word :
Oh ! may that beating heart and ear be fill'd
With one deep whisper, ' Jesus Christ is Lord ! '
And as both Jew and Christian take their turn
To gaze, with kindly interchange of place,
Led up by Love, may hood-winkt Faith return,
Clear of the Talmud, and with open face ;
For Charity shall pave the way for Grace,
The pupil of pure love is quick to learn.

K

XCV.

THE TELEGRAPH CABLE TO INDIA.

Anticipative.

How all the old ways of intercourse have ceased,
Or well-nigh ceased—and we have lived to see
The word of England rapt into the East
Beneath the rolling waters !   Can it be ?
Yea, and thro' lawless regions which we guard
And subsidize ; the Arab and the Turk
Are bound by stress of state, or gross reward,
To aid the mystic courier at its work
Twixt land and sea ; soon, without wave or wind,
Our statesmen shall despatch their ' how ' and ' why '—
And charge the lightning with their policy ;
Nor shall our home-affections lag behind ;
For all that longs, and loves, and craves reply,
Shall move the needle on the shores of Ind.

XCVI.

THE SOUTH-FORELAND ELECTRIC LIGHT.

From Calais pier I saw a brilliant sight,
And from the sailor at my side besought
The meaning of that fire, which pierced the night
With lustre, by the foaming billows caught.
''Tis the South Foreland!' I resumed my gaze
With quicker pulse, thus, on the verge of France,
To come on England's brightness in advance!
There! on the waters! In those far-seen rays
I hail'd the symbol of her fame in fight:
But, by a change akin to that which brought
The lightning under rule, the martial thought
Flash'd itself out, transform'd to quiet light;
I turn'd to all the good she did and taught,
Her shining honour and her moral might.

XCVII.

GREATNESS OF ENGLAND.

Full long ere Europe knew the iron road,
The ' Railway ' thunder'd on our English soil ;
There was a trembling in the sea-girt isle,
Where 'Hercules' or mighty 'Samson' trod,
Heavy and swift ; for Nature bore our yoke
Far earlier than elsewhere : we freed the slave
To take the lightning captive ; hearts of oak,
Of closest grain, the stalwart and the brave,
Thrill'd at the touch of science ; letters lent
Their gentle aid to feed the hungry strength
Of British minds with genial nourishment ;
And still these powers bear rule throughout the length
And breadth o' the land.   The thought is rife with
        pride :
Perchance the ebb comes next.   We stand at full of
        tide.

XCVIII.

THE WIND-BOUND MISSION.

'Deep in the West the godless Mormons dwell,
In the far East the Taepings waste and burn,
And stamp the name of Christ on deeds of hell—
Ah me ! for comfort whither shall I turn,
While East and West breed mockeries like these ? '
I turn'd to Livingstone, on Afric's soil
Labouring, and good Mackenzie's holy toil,[1]
And Selwyn praying for the southern seas—
But never thought more tender and sublime
To any bleeding anxious heart was given,
Than when I learn'd that not a wind-bound sail,
Near this rough foreland, waits the favouring gale,
But Christian men observe the vacant time,
Stand in the baffling wind and speak of heaven !

---

[1] Written previous to the Bishop's death.

XCIX.

THE THAW-WIND.

Thro' the deep drifts the south wind breathed its way
Down to the earth's green face ; the air grew warm,
The snow-drops had regain'd their lonely charm ;
The world had melted round them in a day :
My full heart long'd for violets—the blue arch
Of heaven—the blackbird's song—but Nature kept
Her stately order—Vegetation slept—
Nor could I force the unborn sweets of March
Upon a winter's thaw.   With eyes that brook'd
A narrower prospect than my fancy craved,
Upon the golden aconites I look'd,
And on the leafless willows as they waved—
And on the broad leaved, half-thaw'd ivy-tod,
That glitter'd, dripping down upon the sod.

C

AN APRIL DAY.

The lark sung loud ; the music at his heart
Had call'd him early ; upward straight he went,
And bore in nature's quire the merriest part,
As to the lake's broad shore my steps I bent ;
The waterflies with glancing motion drove
Their dimpling eddies in among the blooms
Shed by the flowering poplars from above ;
While, overhead, the rooks, on sable plumes,
Floated and dipt about the gleaming haze
Of April, crost anon by April glooms,
As is the fashion of her changeful days ;
When, what the rain-cloud blots, the sun relumes
O' the instant, and the shifting landscape shows
Each change, and, like a tide, the distance comes and
    goes !

CI.

THE CHARMING OF THE EAST WIND.

Late in the month a rough east wind had sway,
The old trees thunder'd, and the dust was blown ;
But other powers possess'd the night and day,
And soon he found he could not hold his own ;
The merry ruddock whistled at his heart,
And strenuous blackbirds pierced his flanks with song,
Pert sparrows wrangled o'er his every part,
And thro' him shot the larks on pinions strong :
Anon a sunbeam broke across the plain,
And the wild bee went forth on booming wing—
Whereat he feeble wax'd, but rose again
With aimless rage, and idle blustering ;
The south wind touch'd him with a drift of rain,
And down he sank, a captive to the spring !

CII.

SUMMER EVENING. RETIREMENT OF A GARDEN.

'Scaped from the day's long heats and hustling crowds,
How much for that sweet silence I condoned !
The gold moon glimpsed from out faint-stirring clouds,
And near the nested bird the beetle droned ;
Pensive upon my garden-chair I sat,
And gave my spirit up to evening dreams,
Haunted by fragments of that meagre chat,
That held so long, and touch'd such weary themes,
All worthless !   Near me lay that burial sod
Where to a shining thread such power was given ;
A little, aimless, ferrying, light that stood,
And moved and stood again, at random driven,
But made, by hope, significant for good,[1]
It plies, henceforth, between that hope and heaven.

---

[1] See Sonnet LXIII., page 98.

CIII.

FULVIA,

or

Supposed Thoughts of a Hooted Candidate in his Garden.

Welcome, ye shades of summer eve, that close
My day among the tongues of yonder town !
I would not pluck them out nor pin them down,
As vengeful Fulvia did with Cicero's—
Nor to mere petulance of speech assign
The cruel meed of his rare excellence—
Enough for me this stillness, and the sense
That they no longer vex these ears of mine ;
I will not vent my rage on foolish lungs,
Nor, even in fancy, re-enact the deed
Wreak'd on the Roman, in the stress and need
Of a great anger ; why should ribald songs
Scourge like impeaching eloquence ? or why
Should either tax our needles for reply ?

CIV.

Continued.

'Twas but a moment's ire—the next, withstood—
Yet, in that moment, how my hungry spleen
Ran to the fierce triumvir's wife for food,
Through the long lapse of centuries between !
And, by that ready reference, proved its kin ;
Strange ! how my angry mood sped back through time
To gust my fancy with the ancient crime ;
Impracticable thought ! unwelcome sin !
I gauged again the depth of years, and found
My Master, pleading in His hour of grief,
For friends who did not minister relief,
And foes who mock'd Him, and stood brawling round
His divine silence !—How distinct they were,—
The woman's vengeance and the Saviour's prayer !

CV.

AN APPLICATION OF THE WAXING MOON.

O fair full moon, that did'st embay the dark
With slender horns, when first my vow was made ;
I saw thee grow, half-trustful, half-afraid,
But still prest onward to my goal and mark ;
Hard task was mine ! the true prayer to be pray'd—
The bidding back of all my coward fears—
The ointment to be bought, the homage paid—
The feet of Jesus to be kiss'd with tears.
Yet soon the creeping shade will come again,
And drown thy snowy forelands night by night ;
For thy sole function is to wax and wane :
But faith must keep her victories of light,
Else were it better far to see thee shine,
With comfortable eyes of sheep and kine.

CVI.

THE PLANET AND THE TREE.

The evening breeze is blowing from the lea
Upon the fluttering elm ; thou hast a mind,
O star ! methinks, to settle in the tree—
But, ever baffled by the pettish wind,
Thou movest back and forward, and I find
A pastime for my thoughts in watching thee ;
In thy vast orbit thou art rolling now,
And wottest not how to my human eye
Thou seemest flouted by a waving bough,
Serving my fancy's needs right pleasantly ;
Thou wottest not—but He who made thee knows
Of all thy fair results both far and near,
Of all thine earthly, all thine heavenly shows—
The expression of thy beauty there and here.

CVII.

HESPERUS.

'Shine on the sister planet at thy side,'
The Maker said, when first the worlds were made,
Just as our Hesperus began to glide
Along the path His prescient wisdom laid ;
'Shine on the earth, the home of sin to be ;
The sorrowing eyes of man will need thy light ;
Enter his guilty darkness night by night,
And symbolize his long-lost purity.'
Such is the story of our Evening Star,
As some fond muse might tell it—but, indeed,
'Tis God's own truth that all things near and far
Were made for eyes to see, and hearts to read—
So comes it ever, as the twilights fall,
Sweet Hesperus shines forth for me, for all !

CVIII.

NIGHTINGALES.

What spirit moves the quiring nightingales
To utter forth their notes so soft and clear?
What purport hath their music, which prevails
At midnight, thrilling all the darken'd air?
'Tis said, some weeks before the hen-birds land
Upon our shores, their tuneful mates appear;
And, in that space, by hope and sorrow spann'd,
Their sweetest melodies 'tis ours to hear;
And is it so? for solace till they meet,
Does this most perfect chorus charm the grove?
Do these wild voices, round me and above,
Of amorous forethought and condolence treat?
Well may such lays be sweetest of the sweet,
That aim to fill the intervals of Love!

CIX.

A NIGHT THOUGHT.

O snowy star ! which I all night have eyed,
As some poor girl her lover's moon-lit sail,
Bound for the outer sea at early tide—
The rosy billows and the morning gale—
I grieve to lose thee ! for the night will fail
And thou be gone at dawning ; but, to-night,
Thou fill'st my cup of tears with silver light,
And lustres of regret serene and pale :
Thou dost express and symbolize the whole
Of those deep thoughts that pierce me and refine ;
But see ! the daytime comes with all its dole !
Ah ! woody hills and autumn-tints divine !
Ah ! mournful eyes !   Ah ! sad poetic soul !
Ah ! beauteous thoughts and fatal woes of mine !

CX.

RESUSCITATION OF FANCY.

The edge of thought was blunted by the stress
Of the hard world ; my fancy had wax'd dull,
All nature seem'd less nobly beautiful,—
Robb'd of her grandeur and her loveliness ;
Methought the Muse within my heart had died,
Till, late, awaken'd at the break of day,
Just as the East took fire and doff'd its gray,
The rich preparatives of light I spied ;
But one sole star—none other anywhere—
A wild-rose odour from the fields was borne :
The lark's mysterious joy fill'd earth and air,
And from the wind's top met the hunter's horn ;
The aspen trembled wildly, and the morn
Breathed up in rosy clouds, divinely fair !

CXI.

THE FOREST GLADE.

As one dark morn I trod a forest glade,
A sunbeam enter'd at the further end,
And ran to meet me thro' the yielding shade—
As one, who in the distance sees a friend,
And, smiling, hurries to him ; but mine eyes,
Bewilder'd by the change from dark to bright,
Received the greeting with a quick surprise
At first, and then with tears of pure delight ;
For sad my thoughts had been—the tempest's wrath
Had gloom'd the night, and made the morrow gray ;
That heavenly guidance humble sorrow hath,
Had turn'd my feet into that forest-way,
Just when His morning light came down the path,
Among the lonely woods at early day.

CXII.

THE PROCESS OF COMPOSITION.

An Illustration.

Oft in our fancy an uncertain thought
Hangs colourless, like dew on bents of grass,
Before the morning o'er the field doth pass ;
But soon it glows and brightens ; all unsought
A sudden glory flashes thro' the dream,
Our purpose deepens and our wit grows brave,
The thronging hints a richer utterance crave,
And tongues of fire approach the new-won theme ;
A subtler process now begins—a claim
Is urged for order, a well-balanced scheme
Of words and numbers, a consistent aim ;
The dew dissolves before the warming beam ;
But that fair thought consolidates its flame,
And keeps its colours, hardening to a gem.

CXIII.

MORNING.

It is the fairest sight in Nature's realms,
To see on summer morning, dewy-sweet,
That very type of freshness, the green wheat,
Surging thro' shadows of the hedgerow elms ;
How the eye revels in the many shapes
And colours which the risen day restores !
How the wind blows the poppy's scarlet capes
About his urn ! and how the lark upsoars !
Not like the timid corn-craik scudding fast
From his own voice, he with him takes his song
Heavenward, then, striking sideways, shoots along,
Happy as sailor boy that, from the mast,
Runs out upon the yard-arm, till at last
He sinks into his nest, those clover tufts among.

CXIV.

THE LATTICE AT SUNRISE.

As on my bed at dawn I mused and pray'd,
I saw my lattice prankt upon the wall,
The flaunting leaves and flitting birds withal—
A sunny phantom interlaced with shade ;
'Thanks be to heaven,' in happy mood I said,
'What sweeter aid my matins could befall
Than this fair glory from the East hath made?
What holy sleights hath God, the Lord of all,
To bid us feel and see ! we are not free
To say we see not, for the glory comes
Nightly and daily, like the flowing sea ;
His lustre pierceth through the midnight glooms ·
And, at prime hour, behold ! He follows me
With golden shadows to my secret rooms ! '

CXV.

WIND ON THE CORN.

Full often as I rove by path or stile,
To watch the harvest ripening in the vale,
Slowly and sweetly, like a growing smile—
A smile that ends in laughter—the quick gale
Upon the breadths of gold-green wheat descends ;
While still the swallow, with unbaffled grace,
About his viewless quarry dips and bends—
And all the fine excitement of the chase
Lies in the hunter's beauty : In the eclipse
Of that brief shadow, how the barley's beard
Tilts at the passing gloom, and wild-rose dips
Among the white-tops in the ditches rear'd :
And hedgerow's flowery breast of lacework stirs
Faintly in that full wind that rocks the outstanding firs.

CXVI.

HARVEST-HOME.

Late in September came our corn-crops home,
Late, but full-ear'd—by many a merry noise
Of matron and of maid, young girls and boys,
Preceded, flank'd and follow'd, did they come ;
A general joy ! for piles of unwrought food
For man and beast, on those broad axles prest,
And strain'd those sinewy necks in garlands drest ;
The harebell and the ragwort wondering stood
As the slow teams wound up that grassy lane ;
All knew the husbandman's long task was done ;
While, as they crost his disk, the setting sun
Blazed momently betwixt each rolling wain
And that which follow'd, piled with golden grain,
As if to gratulate the harvest won.

CXVII.

CEASING OF THE STORM.

The storm had well nigh gone ; no fitful blast
Lifted the weeping willow into heaven,
To let it fall and weep again, downcast ;
How often is such fickle comfort given !
How peaceful seem'd the far up floating rook,
Crossing with jetty wing the full white cloud,
As to the blue beyond his way he took ;
While, in the grove, a lingering breeze allow'd
The sight to catch, 'mid play of wind and sun,
The uncertain shadows of that woodland nook,
Swallowing the silent shafts of light that run
Along the spider's thread ; on nature's book
I love to pore, and mark what soars on high,
Or lurks in bye-paths for the observant eye.

CXVIII.

TIME AND TWILIGHT.

In the dark twilight of an autumn morn,
I stood within a little country-town,
Wherefrom a long acquainted path went down
To the dear village haunts where I was born ;
The low of oxen on the rainy wind,
Death and the Past, came up the well-known road,
And bathed my heart with tears, but stirr'd my mind
To tread once more the track so long untrod ;
But I was warn'd, 'Regrets which are not thrust
Upon thee, seek not ; for this sobbing breeze
Will but unman thee ; thou art bold to trust
Thy woe-worn thoughts among these roaring trees,
And gleams of by-gone playgrounds—Is't no crime
To rush by night into the arms of Time ?'

CXIX.

DREAMS.

Most dreams are like the tide upon the beach
Rolling the baseless pebbles, till their place
Is changed and changed again, beyond the reach
Of the best waking memory to retrace
The loose and helpless motion ; these, and those
That stand like rocks, engraved with name and date,
And cognizable words of coming fate,
What mean they? who among our schoolmen
    knows ?
What means this double power to rave and teach?
This common fund of toys and verities?
Of dooming oracles and foolish cries?
Now kept apart, now blending each with each—
Abortive interests, and unreal ties,
And prophecies no daylight can impeach !

CXX.

THE MARBLE LANDING.

An Incident at Spezzia.

They sunk a graven stone into the ground
Where first our Garibaldi's ship was moor'd,
Whereon an angry record of his wound
Beneath those fair memorial lines, was scored ;
At night the accusing tablet was replaced
By one, discharged of that injurious word,
That pierced the general bosom like a sword,
Belied their love, their common hope disgraced.
Lie firm, thou latest-written rock ! his meed
Of honour should be neighbour'd by no groan
Of party spleen—perish the bitter seed
In the pure marble furrow vainly sown !
Why brand with purposed hate a casual deed
That made our hero's noble patience known?

CXXI.

THE LANDING OF KING GEORGE I. OF GREECE AT THE PIRÆUS.

Nature and man should join with one accord
To celebrate this purer second birth
Of royalty—blue skies and Attic mirth,
And boughs of myrtle round the guardian sword ;
A double strength of purple on the hills,
And a wine-fount in mid-Athens ! that each mouth
May quaff the young king's health, and slake the
  drouth
Of that long-drawn Bavarian term of ills ;
And you, Ionian Isles ! when Adria's wave
Comes foaming in before the Danish prows,
Remember England, ruling but to save,
And how she listen'd to your earnest vows ;
Remember England in that night's carouse,
For what her mighty hand, unfolding, gave

CXXII.

TO A FRIEND.

My low deserts consist not with applause
So kindly—when I fain would deem it so,
My sad heart, musing on its proper flaws,
Thy gentle commendation must forego ;
As toys, which, glued together, hold awhile,
But, haply brought too near some searching fire,
Start from their frail compacture, and beguile
The child, that pieced them, of his fond desire :
I was a very child for that brief tide,
Whenas I join'd and solder'd thy good word
With my poor merits—'twas a moment's pride—
The flames of conscience sunder'd their accord :
My heart dropt off in sorrow from thy praise,
Self-knowledge baulk'd self-love so many ways.

CXXIII.

ALEXANDER THE GREAT'S DESIGNS AT BABYLON FRUSTRATED.

He plied Hephæstion's ear with royal schemes
Over the wine-cup ; hollow rang his voice
From barrier-rocks of Providence, and gleams
Of fatal fever lighten'd from his eyes ;
He thought to build and drain with busy power—
But could not pass beyond the appointed goal ;
For the strong ward of one prophetic scroll
Had fray'd the horns of Ammon, and his hour
Drew nigh ; Time sped—the bitterns throng'd the
          strand,
And shook the site of his imperial dream
With booming, and the dropsy of the land
Grew from the untended waters ; evening's beam,
And morn's, look'd down upon a realm of fear,
With pools and mounds and marshes far and near.

CXXIV.

*JULIAN'S ATTEMPT TO BUILD ON THE
SITE OF THE TEMPLE.*[1]

The crowd is climbing up the sacred hill
With loud acclaim and music—shall we see
Jehovah's irreversible decree
Dogg'd into hiding by the Roman's will?
Shall this proud king our Lord's own words gainsay?
Nay—by that burst of sudden fire which sears
The uplifted hand of labour! by the fears
Of that vast crowd! By Christ and Moses, nay!
The Apostate challenged God on His own ground;
And as His prophet struck the fifties down,
The baffled servants of that older crown—
So now His flames their dazzled sense confound;
For none but He, who did the like before,
Shall change the story of Araunah's floor.

---

[1] This sonnet is placed before the one which speaks of
Diocletian, irrelevant to the chronology, and merely as a pendant
to the first: both recording abortive attempts to defeat the
Divine decrees; though of course Alexander put himself in no
conscious opposition to them. These two sonnets, being written
independently of, and therefore with but a loose relevancy to
the rest, may still be considered as, in some sort, introductory
to the series.

CXXV.

TERMINUS.[1]

Upon the roll of folly and of crime
Their lives a fact, for intellectual scorn—
But more for Christian pity, so forlorn
And abject stands it in the stream of Time !
The Imperial mandate ran, that, on a day
Held sacred to the Lord of limitations,
The Christian faith should have its conquering way
Barr'd up, and so the disenchanted nations
Go back to Jove and Phœbus and the fanes ;
Messiah ! and the block-God Terminus !
O stolid humour !   O elaborate pains,
All lost and wasted ! for it is not thus
That truth is stopt ; Saints bled, but idols fell,
The Church bow'd eastward still, and all was well.

---

[1] The feast of the Roman God 'Terminus,' who presided over boundaries, had been selected to be the day beyond which Christianity should be unknown.—*Wilberforce's Five Empires,* from *Lactantius de M. P. XVII.*

CXXVI.

MODERN TERMINI.

Again we see the obstructive rites decreed—
This time by modern schools, a wrangling lot ;—
Each hopes his little god shall do the deed,
The glorious deed—which Terminus did not !
The master lectures, and the pupils quote,
And noise abroad each fire-new theory,
Or stale old sophism.   How they rave and dote !
And plant their idols where their Lord should be !
Soon may we say, ' the heathen dream is past !
The worship of these human blocks of stone,
These heirs of Terminus, is failing fast !
By history and reason overthrown ;
On their hard fronts the sunrise strikes in vain,
No Memnon-chords have they in all their sorry grain ! '

M

CXXVII.

CHRIST AND ORPHEUS.

What means this vain ideal of our Lord,
With 'Orpheus' underwritten ?   Couldst thou see
With eyes of faith the Incarnate Deity,
That faith a nobler title would accord
Than this, whereat no Christian fancy warms ;
Thou would'st not score the mythic harper's name
Beneath the fallen head and outstretch'd arms,
Nor seem to blink our dear Redeemer's claim
To His own cognizance and proper fame ;
The sorrowing manhood of the King of kings,
The double nature, and the death of shame,
The tomb—the rising—are substantial things,
Irrelevant to Orpheus ; What hath made
Thy wisdom match Messias with a shade ?

CXXVIII.

Continued.

O give thy King no bynames ! nor decry
The title proper to His native throne
Within our hearts, as tho' thou would'st deny
The authentic angel's voice which made it known ;
'Tis treason to invalidate our creed
By understatements, partial, vague, and scant ;
A faith in music is not what we want,
This sweet-toned mythus meets no sinner's need ;
Come to the rescue, all who would not fuse
Redemption into harp-notes ! nor exchange
For this new style our grand prescriptive use ;
Nor seek, from flying leaves of legend strange,
To annotate Christ Jesus ! till the next
Bold pen obtrudes the margin on the text.

CXXIX.

Continued.

O friend, it is a deep religious loss
To palter with our Master's pure renown ;
To lose the sad precision of the Cross
In Fancy's lights, and melt away His crown ;
Gazing on truth, why should our vision swim ?
Let Calvary stand clear of fabulous mist,
Keep all the paths of Olivet for Christ,
And let no Orphic phantom walk with Him !
Then, and *then only*, welcome ! what they tell
Of that majestic harp, which came full-strung
Among the woes of Hades, to compel
A pause in all her penance—of the spell
Marr'd by a look—and of that faithful tongue,
Which Death and Hebrus strove in vain to quell.

CXXX.

ON CERTAIN BOOKS.

Faith and fixt hope these pages may peruse,
And still be faith and hope ; but, O ye winds !
Blow them far off from all unstable minds,
And foolish grasping hands of youth !   Ye dews
Of heaven ! be pleased to rot them where they fall,
Lest loitering boys their fancies should abuse,
And they get harm by chance, that cannot choose ;
So be they stain'd and sodden, each and all !
And if, perforce, on dry and gusty days,
Upon the breeze some truant leaf should rise,
Brittle with many weathers, to the skies,
Or flit and dodge about the public ways—
Man's choral shout, or organ's peal of praise
Shall shake it into dust, like older lies.

CXXXI.

Continued.

Alas ! my friend, 'tis motive power one needs
And not these idle fancies ill-advised ;
Mere harness will not pull us up to Christ,
Without the strength of full and living creeds ;
These shiny morals are no match for sin,
These empty trappings are not force nor speed ;
What ! shall we hope the chariot race to win
With straps and head-stalls only ?   To succeed
In that great race, to Faith alone is given—
On-looking Faith, whose object fires the will ;
And, as the distance shrinks 'twixt earth and heaven,
Glows with its motion, and bears forward still,
Because it marks the goal with steadfast eye,
While smart theosophies lose heart and die.

CXXXII.

A DREAM.

I dream'd a morning dream—a torrent brought
From fruitless hills, was rushing deep and wide :
It ran in rapids, like impatient thought ;
It wheel'd in eddies, like bewilder'd pride :
Bleak-faced Neology, in cap and gown,
Peer'd up the channel of the spreading tide,
As, with a starved expectancy, he cried,
'When will the Body of the Christ come down?'
He came—not It, but He ! no rolling waif
Tost by the waves—no drown'd and helpless form—
But with unlapsing step, serene and safe,
As once He trod the waters in the storm ;
The gownsman trembled as his God went by—
I look'd again, the torrent-bed was dry.

CXXXIII.

A WAKING THOUGHT.

No water-floods shall drown our Lord and King !
Nor shall those ancient organs of report,
His glorious Gospels, prove the tempest's sport ;
What makes me sure of what I boldly sing ?
Not my poor dreams ! tho', as the master wills,
They follow truth in darkness—'tis reveal'd
That no brief torrents, from the fruitless hills,
Shall make an ooze of our historic field,
For all mankind by Christ's own prowess won—
Not my poor dreams ! but all that lies between
That time and this—what is and what hath been—
The long array of all that hath been done
And suffer'd, since the Virgin bore her son—
The facts of ages, and the hopes of men !

CXXXIV.

Continued.

I tax not all with this unmanly hate
Of truth, for purer spirits stand without—
Meek men of reverent purpose, watch and wait,
And gaze in sorrow from the land of doubt.
Yes—gentle souls there be, who hold apart,
And long in silence for the day of grace ;
For deep in many a brave, though bleeding, heart
There lurks a yearning for the Healer's face—
A yearning to be free from hint and guess,
To take the blessings Christ is fain to give :
To all who dare not with their conscience strive,
To all who burn for this most dear success,
Faith shall be born ! and, by her natural stress,
Push through these dark philosophies, and live !

CXXXV.

THE TRANSFIGURATION.

The old 'Paulus' Theory.

A fiction or a fact? an interview
Of Christ with His own prophets? or a blink
Of moonlight caught by dreaming eyes, that wink
And wonder, and report what is not true?
When will the impugners of the Gospel claims
The deep consistent likeness recognise
Between His woes and glories?   Living ties
That bind in one His honours and His shames?
For all coheres ; His pangs and triumphs touch
Each other, like the wings of Cherubim :
Strange was His Birth—His death and rising, such
As to bear out that strangeness—and as much
May well be said of dark Gethsemane,
That sternest link in the great unity.

CXXXVI.

GETHSEMANE.

Pursing his traitor lips he onward went,
The Apostle, with those harsh official men—
All on one cruel baleful thought intent,
To hunt the Lamb up from His sheltering glen,
O cruel conclave ! where those murderers met ;
O vile night-market ! where our Lord was sold
Among the sad gray olives, in His sweat,
Just risen from that awful prayer ; behold !
They lead Him forth, the Victim long foretold
To climb, like Isaac, up the fated hill :
And so God wrought Redemption—fold in fold
With hate and guile He wrapt His holy will,
Yet left that will still holy—nor approved
The sin He work'd with, nor its curse removed

CXXXVII.

THE CRITICS AT GETHSEMANE.

Even here we meet the Critics.   The deep grief,
Which all imaginative Art would faint
To express—the Angel's visit of relief—
The God bow'd earthward like some mourning saint—
They tone down all in their unhappy way ;
Distilling rose-tints from their Saviour's blood,
The God-man's sweat of anguish ! to portray
Their sweet young Syrian—so divinely good,
' We must forgive His worshippers,' they say ;
Not so the Church ! and tho' she needs must blush
At her own feeble handling, yet alway,
When she would paint her Master's darkest day,
She takes the full-hued life-drop on her brush,
And works, in simple faith, as best she may.

CXXXVIII.

THE 'HIGHER CRITICISM.'

O Sophistry ! how many lips have kiss'd
And fondled thy puft hand, bedaub'd with ink
Of the 'higher criticism,' which does not shrink
To substitute, for our sound faith in Christ,
A dreamy, hollow, unsubstantial creed :
Strikes its small penknife through the covenants
Both old and new, and, in a trice, supplants
Without replacing, all we love and need ;
How blank will be thy scholarly regret
To see these blurr'd and shredded Gospels mount
Beyond the knives and ink-horns !—buoyant yet
With native strength, of which thou madest no count,
And, as heaven's lively oracles, confest
By all, disprove, perforce, each lying test.

CXXXIX.

ST. JOHN'S EAGLE.

He holds his course, he stoops not at command,
That stately-soaring Eagle of Saint John !
Though, all-agape, the learned critics stand
To lure him to their fancy-perch, upon
The lower rounds of time ; straight up he soars
From holy Zion ! bound by no Greek rules,
Nor held in leash by Alexandrian schools—
The mind of Christ, not Plato's, he explores ;
Sunward he hies.   Ye sages, clear your ken,
See true for once, and register your sight ;
And in the note-books fretted by your pen,
While yet your eye-balls glow, the vision write :
And, when the unrighteous question stirs again,
Remember what you wrote as thoughtful men !

CXL.

THE LUXOR NATIVITY.

A full-blown, modern, speculative sage
Is on us, cramm'd with Egypt—with his dream
Of Nile he seeks the folds of Bethlehem,
And writes 'from Luxor' on the sacred page;
The 'young child' came from Egypt; yet not so,
As this vain scribe would have it—not the son
Of an old Coptic frieze, but the Holy One
Of Israel, Virgin-born! O shame and woe!
But, O my Church, thou standest ever sure,
Though meteors through thine open portals glow,
Discolouring with strange lights, that come and go,
Thine altars, and thy fonts, and vestments pure—
Flashing their alien tinct on the true grain
Of thy great dogmas—Evermore in vain.

CXLI.

A NON-NATURAL CHRISTMAS.

O Christmas hollies !   O thrice-blessed morn !
Again with thy dear message art thou come,
A word of joy to thousands, but to some
A fable among fables, ' Christ is born ! '
Hold off the hour to which our folly leans,
When priesthood in his own white robe shall stand
Forsworn—amid the faithful evergreens !
A thief—a traitor to his own right hand !
Once perjured and ordain'd, what follows next ?
Whene'er, as preacher, to his flock he speaks,
The self-yoked sophist, fretting at his text,
Will rub against its meaning—while the weeks
And months drag on his hollow Christian year—
Woe to faint hearts ! we must not falter here.

CXLII.

A NON-NATURAL EASTER.

Ill fares the priest to-day, who blinks the faith
Of Easter, and, recoiling from the shock
Of the great theme submitted to his flock,
Reserves his thoughts about the Life and Death;
How false he feels when our high feast returns!
While, in his pulpit, on his sidelong eye
The chalice gleams, the great East window burns,
The snow-white board obtrudes its purity;
And he must go and bless it—yea, he goes!
Though covert ironies within him ask
Whether, in very deed, our Day-star rose;
'Tis sad to see him how he takes his mask
To meet the morning! timid and untrue,
And missing all the sweet airs and the dew!

CXLIII.

A NON-NATURAL ASCENSION AND WHIT-SUNDAY.

Christ leaves to-day the little gazing crowd
Upon the Mount, as straight to Heaven He fares ;
O ! let us follow Him with hymns and prayers
Up to the skirts of that receiving cloud ;
But lo ! the preacher hath no hope, no trust,
Nor can he, 'mid our coming Whitsun songs,
Make common cause with all those fiery tongues
That hail the glories of the Pentecost ;
But, if he ever thought it joy to meet
The faithful—if that memory thrills him yet—
Full surely must he feel some fond regret,
At parting with a creed so grand and sweet ;
A grief, as when forsaken Olivet
Roll'd sadly from beneath the Saviour's feet.

CXLIV.

GERMAN AND FRENCH GOSPELS.

How do these eloquent lecturers of France,
And more uncouth expositors of lame
Teutonic Saviours, on our creeds advance,
And push, in crowds, for Messianic fame !
Some in 'great swaths' of learning and untruth
Utter themselves, and vent, in weary tomes,
Their cruel day-dreams, without pause or ruth,
Staunch to a worse apostacy than Rome's ;
Others, in tenderer tones, our hopes decry,
And blight all careless hearts with moral death,
And, with sweet voices, summon us to die ;
But, all alike, reduce our grand old faith,
Our full-orb'd creeds, to merest nuclei,
With atmospheres of philosophic breath !

CXLV.

LEBEN JESU AND VIE DE JÉSUS.

Hail, ancient creeds! that help us to disdain
These ' Lives of Jesus ;' you, that boldly speak
Of an authentic Saviour, gracious, meek,
And wonderful, the Lamb for sinners slain ;
Well, they may fret weak faith, make rebels glad,
But Oh ! what honest soul can wish to see
These churches of the ' Leben ' or the ' Vie '
Get themselves towers in Christendom ? how sad
Is this wild masque of Christs, that flits athwart
The world, ' lo here ! lo there !' from all the schools,
While the true Lord of glory stands apart,
And bides His welcome, as the madness cools,
When they shall greet Him with fond eyes and heart,
And test His slighted word by holier rules.

CXLVI.

THE YOUNG NEOLOGIST AT BETHLEHEM.

A Recommendatory Letter.

Ye shepherds ! angels now ! who gladly heard
That midnight Word of God, in music given,
Which told of Christ's Nativity, and stirr'd
Your hearts with melodies from middle heaven ;
Tend this poor creedless youth through David's town !
Be ever near him with a silent spell,
And lead him to the spot, where, floating down
Upon your watch, the choral blessing fell !
There charm away his false and flimsy lore,
And breathe into his soul your simple creed,
The child of angels' hymns and good men's heed,
The faith of Jesus Christ, nor less nor more—
So may he all his erring steps retrace,
And bless sweet Bethlehem for her day of grace.

CXLVII.

HOW THE 'HIGHER CRITICISM' BLESSES THE BIBLE.

You say 'tis still God's Book, still true and wise—
Tho' you have shorn it of its noblest parts,
Disparaged all its great biographies,
And left no nourishment for pining hearts ;
But that's a foodless river, where the fish
Are stolen from the waters, every fin,
Whence thieves have harried all that God put in,
And spared us scarce enough to freight a dish ;
So have you stolen away our food for faith—
With Moses disallow'd, and Paul review'd,
And Christ Himself by rival pens pursued,
That race each other thro' His life and death—
It irks my soul to see how bland you look,
Giving your foolish blessing to the Book !

*The following Sonnets, as far as No. CCXXXIV.,
were published in* 1868.

CXLVIII.

MY FIRST AND LAST STROPHE.

On being asked to write an Ode by a Friend.

Dear friend ! I had commenced the ' soaring ode '—
But oh ! I felt, despite thy flattering talk,
Like some poor sparrow, captured by a hawk,
And borne on alien wings from his abode
Beneath the sheltering eaves.   It is an art
Beyond my scope and pitch ; I stare and pant
In this Pindaric clutch, and feel my want
Of force ; henceforth I shall grow faint at heart
To see a falcon tower.   Let lyrics be ;
For, though I do not love to say thee nay,
For my poor muse it is too late a day
To mell with strophe and antistrophe !
When odes are paramount, 'tis best for me
To house and peep, lest I be swoop'd away.

CXLIX.

THE GOLD-CRESTED WREN.

His relation to the Sonnet.

When my hand closed upon thee, worn and spent
With idly dashing on the window-pane,
Or clinging to the cornice—I, that meant
At once to free thee, could not but detain;
I dropt my pen, I left the unfinish'd lay,
To give thee back to freedom; but I took—
Oh, charm of sweet occasion !—one brief look
At thy bright eyes and innocent dismay;
Then forth I sent thee on thy homeward quest,
My lesson learnt—thy beauty got by heart:
And if, at times, my sonnet-muse would rest
Short of her topmost skill, her little best,
The memory of thy delicate gold crest
Shall plead for one last touch,—the crown of Art.

CL.

THE HOLY EMERALD.

Said to be the only true likeness of Christ.

The gem, to which the artist did entrust
That Face which now outshines the Cherubim,
Gave up, full willingly, its emerald dust,
To take Christ's likeness, to make room for Him.
So must it be, if thou wouldst bear about
Thy Lord—thy shining surface must be lower'd,
Thy goodly prominence be chipt and scored,
Till those deep scars have brought His features out :
Sharp be the stroke and true, make no complaints ;
For heavenly lines thou givest earthy grit :
But oh ! how oft our coward spirit faints,
When we are call'd our jewels to submit
To this keen graver, which so oft hath writ
The Saviour's image on His wounded saints !

CLI.

ST. AUGUSTINE AND MONICA.

When Monica's young son had felt her kiss—
Her weeping kiss—for years, her sorrow flow'd
At last into his wilful blood ; he owed
To her his after-life of truth and bliss :
And her own joy, what words, what thoughts could
     paint !
When o'er his soul, with sweet constraining force,
Came Penitence—a fusion from remorse—
And made her boy a glorious Christian saint.
Oh ye, who tend the young through doubtful years
Along the busy path from birth to death,
Parents and friends ! forget not in your fears
The secret strength of prayer, the holy breath
That swathes your darlings ! think how Austin's faith
Rose like a star upon his mother's tears !

CLII.

NEHEMIAH'S NIGHT RIDE.

When Nehemiah rode into the dark,
And stones of ruin cumber'd his advance,
And old localities were hard to mark,
Methinks he spent some moments in a trance
Of sounds from past and future—Abraham's foot
With Isaac's on Moriah; then the sigh
Of Moses, beyond Jordan doom'd to die,
So near the soil wherein his heart had root:
'Ay!' thought he, 'and my own fond suit was met
By earthly and by heavenly sympathy!'
Then came sweet tones from far Gennesaret,
A plash, as from the casting of a net,
The noise as of a Cross grounded and set
Hard by him, and a loud and lonely cry!

CLIII.

SALOME.

How little didst thou think, while tripping down
To meet Herodias, from that wild carouse,
That thou wouldst win such terrible renown,
And men should name thy name with heavy brows!
For, in the fierce light of thy mother's guilt,
Before the nations thou art dancing still
Up to the wine-cups!   Holy life was spilt,
And thy fair girlhood served a murderous will:
And so thou fillest up the historic page
With the keen Scribe and ruthless Pharisee,
And, link'd with all the furies of the age,
Hast found no pitying heart to plead for thee;
For, lo! thy dancing-dress is bloody-red,
And thy young hands have borne John Baptist's head!

CLIV.

Continued.

But didst thou not relent? our pity asks;
Didst thou not shudder at that daring deed?
Though voices from the flagons and the flasks
Bad thee and the slain prophet's head good speed
To the Queen's chamber? Herod rued his oath,
And shudder'd in the net his hands had drawn
About himself, and wish'd his vow unsworn:
And was the tender maiden nothing loth
To lend herself to that foul deed of hate,
Whose issue is the world's eternal blame?
Didst thou not rather bend, in silent shame,
O'er the cold lips, so eloquent of late,
From which the breath of holy anger came
As pure as the wild honey which he ate?

CLV.

CHARLOTTE CORDAY,

A Memoir of a Hand.

A child's small hand, lost in her father's—twined
In springtide round the stems of earliest flowers,
Which she had found in fields and orchard-bowers,
With earnest eyes, that best deserve to find ;
A woman's hand—whose pulses ever glow'd
With eager purpose, running bolder blood
Than childhood's ; though the loving teardrops flow'd
Whene'er she clasped in dreams her country's good :
An armèd hand ! fresh from the stricken throat
Of that fierce homicide, whose rage of heart
Woke counter-rage, that came and saw and smote ;
Ah ! maiden's hand ! blood-stain'd at last ! thou art
The very symbol of the unnatural time
When Norman Charlotte dared her noble crime.

CLVI.

WÖLF AND THE CASKET,

Or the Unity of the Iliad.

Though Wölf, in hypercritic zeal, insists
On breaking up that old Ionian harp,
And parcels out to many melodists
The Chian's lonely fame,—he cannot warp
Our common sense, pervert our natural taste ;
Great Aristotle, and that warrior-youth
Of old, held simpler views of Epic truth ;
Master and pupil felt his unity ;
And, when the monarch in his casket placed
The roll, the verdict of a world he took :
In truth, a plural Homer cannot be !
One Muse maintains the quarrels and the loves
One ardent voice, like Heaven-sent Ossa, moves
The war from fight to fight, from book to book.

CLVII.

PHILOCTETES.

Silent they gaze from Ilion's battlements—
Yon sail to-day has brought her latest foe ;
Silent they gaze upon the plain below,
And hear glad voices from the Grecian tents :
Not now Achilles, shouting from the trench,
Dismays them—but that friend of Hercules,
Arm'd with the Hydra's blood to fight for Greece,
Though once deported for his rueful stench ;
The cruel shafts will soon be on the wing,
So brief is that beleaguer'd city's span ;
The leech has gone to that ill-savour'd man :
The foot of Philoctetes yearns to spring
Like young Protesilàûs !   Troy hath learn'd
Her fate,—the ten-years' exile hath return'd !

CLVIII.

Continued.

PHILOCTETES.

Onward the fatal hours and minutes steal,
To-morrow shall his archery commence,
And Troy's proud walls be left without defence,
Open and mortal as Achilles' heel :
To-morrow that old suitor shall exact
Grim vengeance, now for ten years overdue—
For Menelâûs and Œnone too—
The adulterer shall be slain—the city sackt :
Night falls—The mighty bow lies still on board,
And dips and rises with the heaving wave :
The ship-light flickers on that thirsty hoard
Of arrows, which the twelve-fold labourer gave ;
The night-watch halts beside it, pondering all
The dreadful purport of his chief's recall.

O

CLIX.

ON AN OLD ROMAN SHIELD FOUND IN
THE THAMES.

Drown'd for long ages, lost to human reach,
At last the Roman buckler reappears,
And makes an old-world clang upon the beach,
Its first faint voice for many a hundred years ;
Not the weird noises on the battle-field
Of Marathon, as thrilling legends tell,
Could speak more sadly than this ancient shield,
As ringing at the fisher's feet it fell.
How cam'st thou to be grappled thus, and haul'd
To shore, when other prey was sought, not thou?
How strangely was thy long-lost chime recall'd,
As when the arrows struck thee !   Then, as now,
The tented plain was throng'd with armèd men ;
Our weapons change, we quarrel now as then !

CLX.

ON THE SAME.

He drew it home—he heaved it to the bank—
No modern waif, but an old Roman targe ;
The mild familiar swan in terror shrank
From the rude plash, and left the weltering marge.
Low rang the iron boss ; the fisher stared
At his new capture, while, in mystic tones,
The lost shield call'd its legion, whose death-groans
And clash of onset it had seen and heard.
Oh ! when shall better thoughts be dear to man,
Than rapine and ambition, fraud and hate ?
Oh ! when shall War, like this old buckler, fall
Into disuse, drown'd by its own dead weight ?
And Commerce, buoyant as the living swan,
Push boldly to the shore, the friend of all ?

CLXI.

THE BIER OF THE CHRISTIAN SOLDIER.

When first the blackthorn blossom'd, thou wast brave
And strong, but April left thee faint and sick ;
The May-wasp dipt into thine open grave,
And struck the velvets of thy hearse—so quick
Thy summons came.   Disease and languor stole
The pulses of thy young heroic hands ;
But thou didst ever bow to Heaven's commands,
And so the act of dying made thy soul
An instant guest in Paradise !   How calm
And still lay those brave hands, which ever yearn'd
For prayer, yet never from the combat turn'd !
Though sunder'd for dispatch of martial deeds,
Each with its weapon, serving fiery needs,
They long'd to press each other, palm to palm.

CLXII.

THE ILLUMINATION OF THE ENGLISH AND FRENCH FLEETS AT PORTSMOUTH.

Thanks to those festal fires ! mankind shall be
All brothers now ! since France and England met,
The far-seen glow of their great amity
Hangs on the world's horizons : they have set
A glorious fashion !   On the illumined flood
Their two great navies, like some mighty raft,
Rode in their oneness ; without spleen or craft,
They met in light—God saw that it was good ;
And, oh ! those long-drawn rockets, how they climb'd,
To fill the very heaven with tricolors !
What healths we drank, by booming cannon timed !
And how the city swarm'd from all her doors
To greet the Frenchman on our English shores !
And how the bells of welcome peal'd and chimed !

CLXIII.

ON A PICTURE OF ARMIDA AND RINALDO,
WITH THE DECOY-NYMPH.

Dear is that picture for my childhood's sake,——
The man asleep, so near to love or harm ;
The wingèd boy, that stays Armida's arm,
The siren-girl, all hush'd, lest he awake ;
While, in the background of that pictured tale,
Sown with enchanted herbs, and clad with gloom,
A sombre eminence o'erlooks the vale,
A purple hill, where all my dreams found room :
'Tis strange, with how few touches of a brush,
That painter's hand supplied, in life's fresh dawn,
The mystic thoughts I loved ! Sweet thoughts ! deep-
    drawn,
Far-destined ; cherish'd still without a blush ;
Deep-drawn—from God's own founts of mystery ;
Far destined—for my soul must ever be.

CLXIV.

ART AND FAITH.

When first I home return'd, and took my part
Once more in rural duties, I had brought
A memory stored with forms of ancient art,
And faithful visions kept them in my thought;
Day after day Apollo stretch'd his arm,
And gazed in triumph, o'er our village road;
While Fancy heard, aloof, the noise of harm,
That reach'd the Python from the Archer-god.
Let me not leave thee, O my Lord, for these,
Nor merge in Art my Christian fealty!
Through all the winsome sculptures of old Greece
Keep Thou an open walk for Thee and me!
No whiteness is like Thine, All-pure and good!
No marble weighs against Thy precious Blood.

CLXV.

LUCY.

The sculptor carves the stone, till he beholds
Its lessening bulk his finer thought fulfil ;
The flesh and blood our heavenly Artist moulds,
Wax'd fuller, while He wrought it fairer still,
As Lucy grew to woman. Not a girl
In all the village wore her gracious look :
But each her dear pre-eminence could brook,
Nor wish'd a duller gloss on the least curl
Of her bright auburn hair. Love came to woo
In humblest guise, yet no coquettish guile
Depraved the honest beauty of her smile ;
Her goodness raised and better'd those who drew
The lot of the rejected, for they knew
Her utter truth and sweetness all the while !

CLXVI.

MARY—A REMINISCENCE.

She died in June, while yet the woodbine sprays
Waved o'er the outlet of this garden-dell ;
Before the advent of these Autumn days
And dark unblossom'd verdure.   As befel,
I from my window gazed, yearning to forge
Some comfort out of anguish so forlorn ;
The dull rain stream'd before the bloomless gorge,
By which, erewhile, on each less genial morn,
Our Mary pass'd, to gain her shelter'd lawn,
With Death's disastrous rose upon her cheek.
How often had I watch'd her, pale and meek,
Pacing the sward ! and now I daily seek
The track, by those slow pausing footsteps worn,
How faintly worn ! though trodden week by week.

CLXVII.

Continued.

And when I seek the chamber where she dwelt,
Near one loved chair a well-worn spot I see,
Worn by the shifting of a feeble knee
While the poor head bow'd lowly—it would melt
The worldling's heart with instant sympathy:
The match-box and the manual, lying there,
Those sad sweet signs of wakefulness and prayer,
Are darling tokens of the Past to me ;
The little rasping sound of taper lit
At midnight, which aroused her slumbering bird:
The motion of her languid frame that stirr'd
For ease in some new posture—tho' a word
Perchance, of sudden anguish, follow'd it ;
All this how often had I seen and heard !

CLXVIII.

MORNING SORROWS.

Sad memory wakes anew at morning's touch
And, as some muscles move without our will,
She seizes, with involuntary clutch,
The sorrow that we hate, our bosom ill;
But we are form'd with such fine wisdom, such
A Providence our moral need supplies,
That we can seldom overrate our sighs
Nor prize our organs of regret too much;
Then welcome still these ever-new returns
Of anguish! Who escapes or can escape
The burthen, while the great world sins and mourns?
Grief comes to all, whatever be her shape
To each, but we are framed with pain to cope;
And, when we bow, we help our climbing hope.

CLXIX.

MINNIE AND HER DOVE.

Two days she miss'd her dove, and then, alas !
A knot of soft gray feathers met her view,
So light, their stirring hardly broke the dew
That hung on the blue violets and the grass ;
A kite had struck her fondling as he pass'd ;
And o'er that fleeting, downy, epitaph
The poor child linger'd, weeping ; her gay laugh
Was mute that day, her little heart o'ercast.
Ah ! Minnie, if thou livest, thou wilt prove
Intenser pangs—less tearful, though less brief ;
Thou'lt weep for dearer death and sweeter love,
And spiritual woe, of woes the chief,
Until the full-grown wings of human grief
Eclipse thy memory of the kite and dove.

CLXX.

EUSTACE AND EDITH,

Or the old Rocking-horse.

Poor rocking-horse ! Eustace, and Edith too,
Mount living steeds : she leans her dainty whip
Across thy smooth-worn flank, and feels thee dip
Beneath the pressure, while she dons a shoe,
Or lifts a glove, and thinks ' My childhood's gone ! '
While the young statesman, with high hopes possest,
Lays a light hand upon thy yielding crest,
And rocks thee vacantly and passes on.
Yet they both love thee—nor would either brook
Thine absence from this hall, tho' other aims
And interests have supplanted thy mute claims,
And thou must be content with casual look
From those, who sought thee once with earnest will,
And gallop'd thee with all their might and skill.

CLXXI.

Continued.

MAKE-BELIEVE HUNTING.

How often, when the Meet was at the hall,
Those babes took horse, and, in their joy and pride,
Drew half the coverts of the country side;
Sweet innocents! for little Spot was all
Their kennel; hapless Reynard never knew
How wide a field his enemies embraced,
How both in fact and fancy he was chased,
And what that staunch old rocking-horse could do!
Oh! give him kindly greeting, man and maid,
And pat him, as you pass, with friendly hands,
In that dim window where disused he stands,
While o'er him breaks the limewalk's flickering shade;
No provender, no mate, no groom, has he—
His stall and pasture is your memory.

CLXXII.

THE SCHOOL-BOY'S DREAM ON THE NIGHT BEFORE THE HOLIDAYS.

'Twas the half-year's last day, a festal one ;
Light tasks and feast and sport, hoop, cricket, kite,
Employed us fully, till the summer-night
Stole o'er the roofs of happy Alderton.
Homer indoors, and field-games out of school,
Made medley of my dreams ; for, when I slept,
The quaintest vision o'er my fancy swept,
That ever served the lordship of misrule :
Our hoops through gods and heroes ran a-muck ;
Our kites o'erhung the fleet, a public gaze !
And one wild ball the great Achilles struck——
Oh ! how he tower'd and lighten'd at the stroke !
But, tho' his formal pardon I bespoke,
I told him plainly 'twas our holidays.

CLXXIII.

THE ROGUE'S NIGHTMARE.

One who, the self-same morning, had decoy'd
The widow and her son with glozing talk,
At eve through springing pastures walk'd abroad,
And, after his poor sort, enjoy'd his walk.
That night he dream'd: fresh flowers and April grass
Smother'd his cruel pen ; the white lamb kneel'd
Upon his crafty parchments, sign'd and seal'd
By victim hands ; a babbling stream did pass
Sheer through those written wiles, till that base ink,
Which robb'd the widow's mite, the orphan's dole,
Lost colour.   But that dream-begotten blink
Of damage waked at once his mammon-soul ;
From his keen glance all vernal tokens shrink
While Fraud and Twilight watch the lying scroll.

CLXXIV.

LITTLE PHŒBE,

Or the second gathering of the Sea-shells.

The rain had pour'd all day, but clear'd at night,
When, with her little basket on her arm,
She left the door-step of that seaside farm ;
The weeping tamarisk glisten'd in the light,
And chanticleer's green feathers softly waved
Against the dying sunshine.   Forth she fared,
Our host's sweet child, his Phœbe golden-hair'd,
To gather shells, wherewith the beach was paved ;
At dusk, she took the homeward path that led
Beneath yon dark-blue ridge, when, sad to tell,
On her fair head the gloomy Lias fell,
Crumbled by storms,—they found her bruised and
    dead :
Her basket-store was scatter'd by the fall,
But loving hands replaced and kept them all.

P

CLXXV.

ALICE WADE VERSUS SMALL-POX.

Thy golden hair is left—its silky mesh
The spoiler shall not mar, whate'er he takes ;
Nor that still-brilliant eye, that sleeps and wakes
Among the flowing sores : but thy fair flesh,
All-confluent now, and molten by disease,
Must keep the stamp which this sick fortnight gave
Even till that latest fusion in the grave
Runs off our ingrain'd evils ; but for these
Sweet relics of thyself, and what thou wert
A brief moon since, I should be half afraid
That Love might shrink, and merry Hymen flirt
His robe at thy lost hopes, my little maid !
Thou smilest ! Ah ! I see no power can hurt
The fortunes or the loves of Alice Wade !

CLXXVI.

ELLEN,

Or First Love and Death.

That summer dawn, to Love and Edwin dear,
Her sky-blue gown, her happy tears and smiles ;
And the broad harvests, stirring far and near,
And softly floating to the gates and stiles ;
The meadow-sweet and wild rose dew-besprent,
And her pure words of troth, where are they now ?
And the gay lark, that rose at once, and spent
His morning-music on her earliest vow ?
He treads the sodden grass with weary foot
At twilight, weeping for his promised bride :
The wind blows cold ; the corn has long been cut ;
And, three moons since, his plighted Ellen died !
But lo ! that glimmer in the watery rut !
It is a star—in Heaven, yet by his side.

CLXXVII.

ANNIE AND AMBROSE,

Or a Winter-Grove with a Summer-Memory.

Seldom we see such crude cold winter times ;
Yon sooty patch upon the snow-clad weald—
Is that, indeed, the bower of honied limes ?
The balm-grove, where a ten-years' wound was heal'd ?
Where Annie sat with Ambrose ? where she tried
A cure more sweet than Gilead's pharmacy ?
And did she read him his rich destiny
In that dark holt that blurs the white hill-side ?
The brook, I trow, is bound in frosty bands,
Where Rover plash'd, and, venting merry tones,
Trod in the summer-light that swam the sands ;
While, sportive in their bliss, those plighted ones
Confused his eager ear with dropping stones,
But evermore reclasp'd their happy hands.

CLXXVIII.

GOING HOME,

Or a Death in the Thebaid.

The ancient river glimmer'd in its bed,
High overhead the stars of Egypt burn'd,
When our slow-dying Edith join'd the dead ;
She whom the Arab and the Nubian mourn'd :
How in the shadow of old Thebes we wept,
And down the long-drawn Nile from day to day !
Her sweet face gone—her bright hair hid away—
Save what the ring or gleaming locket kept ;
And, when we felt the Midland waters rise
Beneath our keel, and England nearer come—
'Mid our forecasting questions and replies,
Back came the sorrow like a sad surprise ;
Those dear white cliffs would never greet her eyes,
Nor her cheek flush, to find herself at home.

CLXXIX.

JEALOUSY.

Alas! sad Jealousy! the scalding tear
Drops on her hands—her brow aches sadly too;
This morn she wander'd half the country through,
Weeping, with those false eyes for ever near:
She, who look'd boldly in the front of Love,
And search'd his glittering face, so proud and fair,
Must droop her gaze, declining from above,
And clasp his feet, and shed her sorrows there:
Or, like some aged lazar must she lie,
Some palsied crone, who hath no voice but tears—
Who sees the long-expected leech pass by
Her couch, to whisper hope in younger ears;
And her heart trembles, dying, yet astir;
She knows the healer can do nought for her!

CLXXX.

THE HALF-RAINBOW.

The groups of Autumn flowers were all ablaze ;
The hollyhock and scarlet crane's-bill burn'd
Like merry household fires ; but when he turn'd
To search the distance, all was block'd with haze ;
Then came a brightness over rick and roof ;
He gladden'd, as the running sunshine laugh'd
Its way from sheaf to sheaf, while, high aloof,
The rainbow linger'd in one glorious shaft ;
Then, in that light of promise, he appeal'd,
To her who was his heart's best hope ; she heard
The tender suit his trembling lips preferr'd,
And in imperfect words her love reveal'd ;
Her faltering accents gave a pledge divine,
Like Heaven's half-bow, a true tho' broken sign.

CLXXXI.

THE PARTING-GATE.

In that old beech-walk, now bestrewn with mast,
And roaring loud—they linger'd long and late ;
Harsh was the clang of the last homeward gate
That latch'd itself behind them, as they pass'd—
Then kiss'd and parted.   Soon her funeral knell
Toll'd from a foreign clime ; he did not talk
Nor weep, but shudder'd at that stern farewell ;
'Twas the last gate in all their lovers'-walk
Without the kiss beyond it !   Was it good
To leave him thus, alone with his sad mood,
In that dear footpath, haunted by her smile ?
Where they had laugh'd and loiter'd, sat and stood ?
Alone in life ! alone in Moreham wood !
Through all that sweet, forsaken, forest-mile !

CLXXXII.

HERO AND LEANDER,

Or the Boy's Hellespont.

No colder local records did I crave,
Two lovers' names were all my Hellespont;
How oft, methought, the swimming youth was wont
To kiss the waters, where the lighted wave
Came trembling out from Sestos! When the gale
Dimm'd his fond eyes, and chill'd each supple limb,
I broke my heart for both, without avail,
I wept with her! I sobb'd and sank with him!
And if, at times, the historic muse would fill
The strait with forms more secular and vast,
The torch of Hero lived behind them still!
And wide-spread sails of war ran glowing past
Love's watch-fire, till, again, the impassion'd light
Burst on the lonely swimmer, doubly bright.

CLXXXIII.

DROWNED IN THE TROPICS.

The Mother's Questions.

Drown'd, say you? Tell me, tell me, how she fares,
My drown'd one? Has she met the finny shoal?
And roll'd into that glancing march of theirs
Her attitudes of death, with no control
Of living will? Perchance, her feeble form
Falters about wild headlands in the dark,
Where no expectant mother's voice bids ' Hark!
'Tis our own Mary!' Or the tropic storm,
With its fierce lightning rends her lonely face;
Or waterspouts, with writhing motion, suck
At her dear relics; prey-birds. bless their luck
To find her; or the shark and sea-dog trace
From far my fair-eyed fondling—cruel chase
After a helpless prey, already struck!

CLXXXIV.

Continued.

THE SEA-FAIRIES' ANSWER.

Our spells shall keep her floating, yet unchanged ;
The nautilus shall push his purple sail
Across her happy shadow ; in the gale
The storm-blown land-bird, which too far hath ranged,
Shall trust her look, and perch, and close his eye :
Around her shall the graceful pròas move,
And fling their garland gifts of awe and love ;
And, when the tropic midnight veils the sky,
On fair phosphoric seas thy child shall rest,
And morn shall find her, when the day comes back,
Laid, as in Heaven's own river, in the track
Of sunrise o'er the waters—to suggest
In symbol, that her soul is pure and blest,
And floats from light to light, and cannot die.

CLXXXV.

VIENNA AND IN MEMORIAM.

Roused by the war-note, in review I pass'd
The polities of nations—their intrigues—
Their long-drawn wars and hates—their loves and
    leagues ;
But when I came on sad Vienna, last,
Her scroll of annals, timidly unroll'd,
Ran backward from my helpless hands ! the woe
Of that one hour that laid our Arthur low,
Made all her chronicle look blank and cold :
Then turn'd I to that Book of memory,
Which is to grieving hearts like the sweet south
To the parch'd meadow, or the dying tree ;
Which fills with elegy the craving mouth
Of sorrow—slakes with song her piteous drouth,
And leaves her calm, though weeping silently !

CLXXXVI.

TO A LITTLE CHILD WHO ASKED FOR A LAUREL CROWN.

The laurels with their heritage of light,
So thickly planted in our garden-ground,
Like thee, in winter time make all things bright,
And strike each other with a cheery sound.
Well, then !   Of these a garland shall be made
Just for the nonce, for they are fresh and green ;
But soon a gayer coronal I'll braid,
When Summer comes to match thy merry mien :
Woodbine and jessamine shall then enclose
Thy fair young head, well woven with choicest art ;
And many a sprig of verdure interpose,
And pinks and rich carnations bear their part,
White lilies, and the hollow balmy rose,
And pansy, with the day-spring at her heart.

CLXXXVII.

A RECANTATION.

To the same little Child.

The conqueror's chaplet doth not suit at all
Those girlish azure orbs, and tresses' flow :
Above—the victor wreath of ravaged Gaul—
The fairy-land of thy sweet face below,
Unscathed and clear !   Ill fancy ! that I wrought
A garland for thee of such stern device ;
I made a monster, Katie, when I brought
The Cæsar's shadow o'er thy sunny eyes ;
But I must kiss thee, darling, all the same ;
What, peevish ! and this one brief kiss my dole !
Well—as it seems but half a kiss I stole,
Now thou art but half Katie, I will claim
The other half when thou art Katie whole,
Uncrost by martial hints and Roman fame.

CLXXXVIII.

LITTLE SAMUEL,

Or Light and Gloom by the Fireside.

These changes at our weather-wisdom mock ;
But yesterday, the lord of all the year
Upon the front of this white marble clock
Sat like a star of honour, keen and clear,
Small as a spark : to-day, the mantelshelf
And time-piece mirror not his living beams ;
Nought but wan window-lights and pallid gleams,
Where burn'd, in miniature, the Sun himself !
Then frost, now cloudy thaw.   In gilded coat
Above the clock, the infant Samuel kneels
In shine or shade, or when the thunder peals,
He lifts his praying hands and murmurs not :
Oh ! may such holy temper be my lot,
Whatever mood each passing day reveals !

CLXXXIX.

A BRILLIANT DAY.

O keen pellucid air ! nothing can lurk
Or disavow itself on this bright day ;
The small rain-plashes shine from far away,
The tiny emmet glitters at his work ;
The bee looks blithe and gay, and as she plies
Her task, and moves and sidles round the cup
Of this spring flower, to drink its honey up,
Her glassy wings, like oars that dip and rise,
Gleam momently.   Pure-bosom'd, clear of fog,
The long lake glistens, while the glorious beam
Bespangles the wet joints and floating leaves
Of water-plants, whose every point receives
His light ; and jellies of the spawning frog,
Unmark'd before, like piles of jewels seem !

CXC.

THE STARLING,

Or Nest-talk and Fear-talk.

Poor bird ! why with such energy reprove
My presence ? why that tone which pines and grieves ?
At early dawn, thy sweet voice from the eaves
Hath gone between us oft, a voice of love,
A bond of peace.   Why should I ever plot
Thy ruin, or thy fond affections baulk ?
Dost thou not send me down thy happy talk
Even to my pillow, though thou seest me not ?
How should I harm thee ? yet thy timid eye
Is on me, and a harsh rebuke succeeds ;
Not like the tender brooding note that pleads
Thy cause so well, so all-unconsciously ;
Yet shall to-morrow's dawning hear thy strain
Renewed, and knit our indoor bond again.

CXCI.

NO NIGHTINGALES, OR COMPENSATION.

Night of 31st of May.

Long time I waited for the nightingale,
Befool'd by that dumb coppice ; till the dove
And finch descried me watching in the grove,
Poor client of the darkness, worn and pale :
But oh ! how often is our frustrate hope
Exchanged by Heaven for unexpected mirth !
Though baulk'd and sleepless, yet I could not mope
'Mid the full matins of the awaken'd earth ;
Bold chanticleer, alighting from his perch,
' The night birds play thee false,' he said—and crow'd ;
' Welcome to truth and day ! '   The lark uprode
And caroll'd.   Thus, amid my weary search
For song in bowers of silence, June was born,
And tuneless night exchanged for choral morn.

CXCII.

THE WOOD-ROSE.

When Wordsworth found those beds of daffodil
Beside the lake, a pleasant sight he saw ;
I came upon a sweetbriar near a rill,
In all its summer bloom, without a flaw :
The set of all its flowers my thought recalls,
And how they took the wind with easy grace ;
They rode their arches, shook their coronals,
And stirr'd their streamers o'er the water's face.
And oh ! to watch those azure demoiselles
Glimpsing about the rosy sprays, that dipt
Among the weeds,—how daintily equipt
They were ! how pure their blue against the pink !
Light, flitting forms, that haunt our ponds and wells,
Seen, lost and seen, along the reedy brink.

CXCIII.

THE HOME-FIELD. EVENING.

'Tis sweet, when slanting light the field adorns,
To see the new-shorn flocks recline or browse;
While swallows flit among the restful cóws,
Their gurgling dew-laps, and their harmless horns;
Or flirt the aged hunter, in his dose,
With passing wing; yet with no thought to grieve
His mild, unjealous, innocent repose,
With those keen contrasts our sad hearts conceive.
And then, perchance, the evening wind awakes
With sudden tumult, and the bowery ash
Goes storming o'er the golden moon, whose flash
Fills and refills its breezy gaps and breaks;
The weeping willow at her neighbour floats,
And busy rustlings stir the wheat and oats.

CXCIV.

MAGGIE'S STAR.

To the White Star on the forehead of a favourite old Mare.

White star ! that travellest at old Maggie's pace
About my field, where'er a wandering mouth,
And foot, that slowly shifts from place to place,
Conduct thee,—East or West, or North or South ;
A loving eye is my best chart to find
Thy whereabouts at dawn or dusk ; but when
She dreams at noon, with heel a-tilt behind,
And pendent lip, I mark thee fairest then ;
I see thee dip and vanish, when she rolls
On earth, supine ; then with one rousing shake
Reculminate ; but, most, thou lovest to take
A quiet onward course—Heaven's law controls
The mild, progressive motion thou dost make,
Albeit thy path is scarce above the mole's.

CXCV.

A SUMMER NIGHT IN THE BEEHIVE.

The little bee returns with evening's gloom,
To join her comrades in the braided hive,
Where, housed beside their mighty honeycomb,
They dream their polity shall long survive.
Still falls the summer night—the browsing horse
Fills the low portal with a grassy sound
From the near paddock, while the water-course
Sends them sweet murmurs from the meadow-ground ;
None but such peaceful noises break the hush,
Save Pussy, growling, in the thyme and sage,
Over the thievish mouse, in happy rage :
At last, the flowers against the threshold brush
In morning airs—fair shines the uprisen sun
Another day of honey has begun !

CXCVI.

THE BEE-WISP.

Our window-panes enthral our summer bees;
(To insect woes I give this little page)—
We hear them threshing in their idle rage
Those crystal floors of famine, while, at ease,
Their outdoor comrades probe the nectaries
Of flowers, and into all sweet blossoms dive;
Then home, at sundown, to the happy hive,
On forward wing, straight through the dancing flies:
For such poor strays a full-plumed wisp I keep,
And when I see them pining, worn, and vext,
I brush them softly with a downward sweep
To the raised sash—all-anger'd and perplext:
So man, the insect, stands on his defence
Against the very hand of Providence.

CXCVII.

THE FLY'S LECTURE.

Once on a time, when, tempted to repine,
In yon green nook I nursed a sullen theme,
A fly lit near me, lovelier than a dream,
With burnish'd plates of sight, and pennons fine :
His wondrous beauty struck and fixt my view,
As, ere he mingled with the shades of eve,
With silent feet he trod the honeydew,
In that lone spot, where I had come to grieve :
And still, whene'er the hour of sorrow brings,
Once more, the humours and the doubts of grief,
In my mind's eye, from that moist forest-leaf
Once more I see the glorious insect rise !
My faith is lifted on two gauzy wings,
And served with light by two metallic eyes.

CXCVIII.

THE ROOKERY.

Methought, as I beheld the rookery pass
Homeward at dusk upon the rising wind,
How every heart in that close-flying mass
Was well befriended by the Almighty mind :
He marks each sable wing that soars or drops,
He sees them forth at morning to their fare,
He sets them floating on His evening air,
He sends them home to rest on the tree-tops :
And when through umber'd leaves the night-winds
    pour,
With lusty impulse rocking all the grove—
The stress is measured by an eye of love,
No root is burst, though all the branches roar ;
And, in the morning, cheerly as before,
The dark clan talks, the social instincts move.

CXCIX.

ON A VASE OF GOLD-FISH.

The tortured mullet served the Roman's pride
By darting round the crystal vase, whose heat
Ensured his woe and beauty till he died :
These unharm'd gold-fish yield as rich a treat ;
Seen thus, in parlour-twilight, they appear
As though the hand of Midas, hovering o'er,
Wrought on the waters, as his touch drew near,
And set them glancing with his golden power,
The flash of transmutation !   In their glass
They float and glitter, by no anguish rackt ;
And, though we see them swelling as they pass,
'Tis but a painless and phantasmal act,
The trick of their own bellying walls, which charms
All eyes—themselves it vexes not, nor harms.

CC.

THE PLEA OF THE SHOT SWALLOW.

In Teos once, bedew'd with odours fine,
The happy dove slept on his master's lyre ;
A little homelesss swallow clings to mine,
A spirit-bird—he looks for something higher
Than songs and odours ; pity and remorse
He claims—an elegy of words and tears :
He asks me why they swept him from his peers,
When wheeling gaily in his wondrous course ;
And now he comes, with trembling wings, to plead
For some brief record of his cruel fate ;
Some note of tuneful sorrow for the deed
Which struck him from the side of his dear mate.
Poor bird ! had I the Teian's melody,
Sweet as his dainty Ode thy dirge should be.

CCI.

THE LAST SWEEP OF THE SCYTHE.

The year had rush'd along through May and June,
And my own natal month, her goal to win ;
And now the fruitful sheaves were coming in ;
The glow of August made the barren moon
As mellow as the corn-lands.   One bright field,
Which to the southward sloped, enhancing all
The beauty of the view, was last to fall
Before the sweeping scythe.   Its doom was seal'd ;
I grieved to think how fleet and fugitive
Are all our joys, how near to change or harm :
And how that azure distance would outlive
Its golden foreground, losing half its charm !
But I remember'd, ere I look'd again,
That fallen corn is bread, and many a loss true gain.

CCII.

HARVEST-HOME.

All day we watch'd the unintermitted fume
Of clouds, but still there was no downward rush
Of rain ; then evening came and brought a flush
Of windy redness, in the place of gloom ;
None but sweet hues and pleasant airs remain'd ;
The dry light gust that swept the dancing sprays,
And a white moon, astir in rosy haze
Above our latest labours ; none complain'd
Of that sharp toil.   The sheaves flew fast and thick
From fork to fork, to feed the growing rick ;
Each waved its farewell, as it took the leap ;
Some blest the God of harvest, some their luck ;
The horses' weary feet their threshold struck,
And the hinds supt, and slept a happy sleep.

CCIII.

THE STORM—A HARVEST MEMORY.

The specialties of that dark hour of grief
On my retentive heart have prest their seal ;
Yes ! I remember even the spider's wheel,
Which stretch'd and lighten'd on the gusty leaf
Of that wild August morn ! The blasts were driven
Across the new-mown fields, fitful and brief,
And toss'd the tresses of the barley-sheaf,
And rode the streaming willow into Heaven :
The features of the tempest, all and each,
I still recall, and shall thy ruthful gaze
Not be remember'd ? nor those winning ways
Which brought my soul within thy pity's reach ?
I keep the natural impress of the hour,
And shall thy loving kindness have less power ?

CCIV.

THE FIRST WEEK IN OCTOBER.

Once on an autumn day as I reposed
Beneath a noon-beam, pallid yet not dull,
The branch above my head dipt itself full
Of that white sunshine momently, and closed;
While, ever and anon, the ashen keys
Dropt down beside the tarnish'd hollyhocks,
The scarlet crane's-bill, and the faded stocks,—
Flung from the shuffling leafage by the breeze.
How wistfully I mark'd the year's decay,
Forecasting all the dreary wind and rain;
'Twas the last week the swallow would remain—
How jealously I watch'd his circling play!
A few brief hours, and he would dart away,
No more to turn upon himself again.

ccv.

FROM HARVEST TO JANUARY.

The hay has long been built into the stack
And now the grain; anon the hunter's moon
Shall wax and wane in cooler skies, and soon
Again re-orb'd, speed on her wonted track,
To spend her snowy light upon the rack
Of dark November, while her brother Sun
Shall get up later for his eight-hours' run
In that cold section of the Zodiac:
Far from the Lion, from the Virgin far!
Then onward through the last dim month shall go
The two great lights, to where the kalendar
Splits the mid-winter; and the feathery snow
Ushering another spring, with falling flakes
Shall nurse the soil for next year's scythes and rakes.

CCVI.

LAST YEAR'S HARVEST.

Since harvest pass'd from out this lonely gate,
Which strains and clatters now in winter's flaw—
With all the merry groups that stirr'd or sate
Among the red wheat, stemm'd with amber straw,
How changed is all the scene! changed by the law
Of death—and I a weary term must wait,
Till once again the seasons reinstate
The glory and the beauty which I saw!
'Twas here I watch'd the mighty landscape stretch'd
To the far hills, through green and azure grades ;
'Twas here I studied all its lights and shades ;
And from this field, one golden morn, I fetch'd
Some hues for those small tablets, where I paint
My sweetest thoughts, ere they wax cold and faint,

CCVII.

THE STEAM THRESHING-MACHINE

With the Straw Carrier.

Flush with the pond the lurid furnace burn'd
At eve, while smoke and vapour fill'd the yard ;
The gloomy winter sky was dimly starr'd,
The fly-wheel with a mellow murmur turn'd ;
While, ever rising on its mystic stair
In the dim light, from secret chambers borne,
The straw of harvest, sever'd from the corn,
Climb'd, and fell over, in the murky air.
I thought of mind and matter, will and law,
And then of him, who set his stately seal
Of Roman words on all the forms he saw
Of old-world husbandry : *I* could but feel
With what a rich precision *he* would draw
The endless ladder, and the booming wheel !

CCVIII.

Continued.

Did any seer of ancient time forebode
This mighty engine, which we daily see
Accepting our full harvests, like a god,
With clouds about his shoulders,—it might be
Some poet-husbandman, some lord of verse,
Old Hesiod, or the wizard Mantuan
Who catalogued in rich hexameters
The Rake, the Roller, and the mystic Van :
Or else some priest of Ceres, it might seem,
Who witness'd, as he trod the silent fane,
The notes and auguries of coming change,
Of other ministrants in shrine and grange,—
The sweating statue, and her sacred wain
Low-booming with the prophecy of steam !

CCIX.

NOVEMBER SUNSHINE AND THE HOUSE-FLIES.

When the dawn struck on Memnon, as they say,
The child of morning answer'd; so the stroke
Of this warm sunshine on the room, awoke
To song those lesser children of the day,
The window-flies; I watch'd each mazy track,
I saw them deftly treading the smooth pane,
Or, haply, flitting with prone wings and back,
To the near cornice, to return again.
Ah! little ones! your joy is brief and vain:
Full soon the brush shall sweep your tiny forms,
Supine and dumb, into the wind and rain;
'Tis sad to be swept out into the storms.
'Twere sadder to revive, and cast about
For foothold, in that roaring world without!

ccx.

THE DRUNKARD'S LAST MARKET.

The taper wastes within yon window-pane,
And the blind flutters, where his fever'd hand
Has raised the sash, to cool his burning brain ;
But he has pass'd away from house and land.
Cheerly and proudly through the gusty dark
The red cock crows ! the new-dropt lambkin tries
His earliest voice in the home-field, while stark
And stiff, on his own bed, the drunkard lies ;
O'erdone by that steep ride, his weary horse
Poises his batter'd feet and cannot feed ;
From the near moorland hill, the brawling force
Calls loudly—but the dead man takes no heed ;
While Keeper howls his notice of alarm,
And thrills with awe the dusky mountain farm.

CCXI.

THE LATE PASTOR OF WOLDSBY EBRIORUM.

A shepherd sleeps where this fair tombstone stands,
Who made on this wild hill his fixt abode—
Who grasp'd in love the drunkard's trembling hands,
And touch'd his heavy heart with thoughts of God ;
He taught his flock by deeds and words and books ;
The peace of many a sober'd hearth he shared :
And many a sottish aspect was prepared
By hope in death, to answer the bright looks
Of their upbearing angels !   Bless his name,
Who purged your grandsires' lives, and still controls
Your own, and saves you from remorse and shame ;
O happy race ! to you in them he came !
O deep infolded blessing ! which unrolls
From sire to son—a charter for your souls !

CCXII.

ON THE ECLIPSE OF THE MOON OF OCTOBER 1865.

One little noise of life remain'd—I heard
The train pause in the distance, then rush by,
Brawling and hushing, like some busy fly
That murmurs and then settles; nothing stirr'd
Beside.   The shadow of our travelling earth
Hung on the silver moon, which mutely went
Through that grand process, without token sent,
Or any sign to call a gazer forth,
Had I not chanced to see; dumb was the vault
Of heaven, and dumb the fields—no zephyr swept
The forest walks, or through the coppice crept;
Nor other sound the stillness did assault,
Save that faint-brawling railway's move and halt;
So perfect was the silence Nature kept.

CCXIII.

*ON AN ANNULAR ECLIPSE OF THE SUN
IN A STORM.*

'To-morrow is the great Eclipse,' we said :
'The moon shall be an island in the sun!'
Though, when we came to gaze, the rack went on
Tumultuously, and all our hopes betray'd;
But, where the scud ran thinner, we perceived
Hustling along, a strange-compounded form,
Half glitter and half gloom—the sun aggrieved,
And the black moon, confederate with the storm
Against mankind. My next thought brought me ease :
Methought, 'A segment of yon hard dark sphere
Shall borrow light for us, and reappear,
Friendly as Hesper,—and, i' the evening breeze,
Wander and flash behind the dusking trees,
Or guide the boatman on yon stormy mere.'

CCXIV.

THE MOON AND SIN, AN ILLUSTRATION.

When the moon's edge grows dim, then blurr'd and
    rough,
And darkness quarries in her lessening orb,
She yields an image, true and stern enough,
Of all those crimes and sorrows, which absorb
Our hope and life ! The thievish shadow sits
On her smooth rim at first, like Adam's sin ;
But soon the encroaching gloom its way doth win,
And with a stealth that never intermits,
Eats out her glory ; but the moon expands
Once more, and brightens to a perfect sphere,
A blessed restoration, full and clear;
So Christ refills our waning world, and stands
For her lost light : O Saviour ever dear!
Soon shall Thy name be known throughout all lands.

CCXV.

ORION.

How oft I've watch'd thee from the garden croft,
In silence, when the busy day was done,
Shining with wondrous brilliancy aloft,
And flickering like a casement 'gainst the sun :
I've seen thee soar from out some snowy cloud,
Which held the frozen breath of land and sea,
Yet broke and sever'd as the wind grew loud—
But earth-bound winds could not dismember thee,
Nor shake thy frame of jewels ; I have guess'd
At thy strange shape and function, haply felt
The charm of that old myth about thy belt
And sword ; but, most, my spirit was possest
By His great Presence, Who is never far
From his light-bearers, whether man or star.

CCXVI.

FANATICISM, A NIGHT-SCENE IN THE OPEN-AIR.

These sectaries deal in parodies of truth—
Their narrow-minded fancies, crude and mean,
Utter'd with gestures wild and words uncouth
In nature's mighty presence, move our spleen,
When they should move our tears. The gale blew loud,
But still the raving and the rant were heard—
Just then I mark'd, how, from a flying cloud,
Orion swiftly drew his belt and sword,
As he would mount to higher heavens, and go
Still further from the earth ! how little dream'd
The hot fanatic, breathing flames and woe,
Of that ineffable contrast ! Stars that gleam'd,
Free winds and fleecy drift, how pure they seem'd,
How alien from the hearts that grovell'd so !

CCXVII.

MISSING THE METEORS, 1866.

A hint of rain—a touch of lazy doubt—
Sent me to bedward on that prime of nights,
When the air met and burst the aërolites,
Making the men stare and the children shout:
Why did no beam from all that rout and rush
Of darting meteors, pierce my drowsèd head?
Strike on the portals of my sleep? and flush
My spirit through mine eyelids, in the stead
Of that poor vapid dream? My soul was pain'd,
My very soul, to have slept while others woke,
While little children their delight outspoke,
And in their eyes' small chambers entertain'd
Far motions of the Kosmos! I mistook
The purport of that night—it had not rain'd.

CCXVIII.

Continued.

A LOOK-OUT FOR THIRTY YEARS.

Oh ! deaf to Science and her faithful words !
I counted on those fires of prophecy
No more than on some flight of midnight birds,
That pass, unheralded, with sudden cry,—
That never travell'd under Humboldt's eye,
Nor owed themselves at Greenwich.   Thirty years
Must pass ere such bright vision reappears,
And then I shall be dead or near to die ;
Or, should my life bridge over that great gap,
I cannot vouch for my decrepit self,
With feeble knees, weak eyes, and velvet cap,
And all my forethought laid upon the shelf ;
But some good youth, or maid, or rosy elf,
Shall set my thin face heavenward, it may hap.

CCXIX.

THE MOORLAND TREE IN THE GARDEN.

Brought from afar but with no studied choice,
And roughly carted, as thou camest to hand,
By the rude peasant,—how we all rejoice
To see thee grown so beautiful and grand!
In thy old site thou mightst have still been poor
And meagre—or, at best, the summer breeze
Had set thee floating on the lonely moor,
No human hearts to teach, no eyes to please:
Kind Heaven foreknew the boon we all received;
For us, the moral of thy drooping boughs—
And, for thyself, how different is thy lot!
From the bare heath, skirted by distant ploughs,
To all this dear home-honour thou has got;
Thou good man's model, lowly though full-leaved!

CCXX.

IN AND OUT OF THE PINE-WOOD.

A Simile.

Beyond the pine-wood all look'd bright and clear—
And, ever by our side, as on we drove,
The star of eve ran glimpsing through the grove,
To meet us in the open atmosphere;
As some fair thought, of heavenly light and force,
Will move and flash behind a transient screen
Of dim expression, glittering in its course
Through many loop-holes, till its face is seen;
Some thoughts ne'er pass beyond their close confines;
Theirs is the little taper's homely lot,
A woodside glimmer, distanced and forgot—
Whose trivial gleam, that twinkles more than shines,
Is left behind to die among the pines;
Our stars are carried out, and vanish not!

CCXXI.

SILENT PRAISE.

O Thou, Who givest to the woodland wren
A throat, like to a little light-set door,
That opens to his early joy—to men
The spirit of true worship, which is more
Than all this sylvan rapture : what a world
Is Thine, O Lord !—skies, earth, men, beasts, and
    birds !
The poet and the painter have unfurl'd
Their love and wonder in descriptive words,
Or sprightly hues—each, after his own sort,
Emptying his heart of its delicious hoards ;
But all self-conscious blazonry comes short
Of that still sense no active mood affords,
Ere yet the brush is dipt, or utter'd phrase
Hath breathed abroad those folds of silent praise !

CCXXII.

A FOREST SUNSET.

Once on a glorious and resplendent eve,
Through copse and underwood my path I broke ;
The shining sun was on the point to leave,
And flash'd through thickets of the pine and oak ;
'Twas sweet to see those vari-colour'd rays
Come pouring through the coverts silently ;
Through little fluttering loop-holes, set ablaze,
Or blinkt, at will, by shifting of an eye ;
That evening's charms were rich and manifold,
Beyond the reach of my best utterance ;
'Twas some kind Providence, no common chance,
Which made mine eyes wink at those wells of gold
Sprung in the glooming leafage, while the dance
Of wilding-boughs was pleasant to behold.

S

CCXXIII.

*WRITTEN AT THE WOOD-SALE OF MESSRS.
BLANK AND CO. NON-RESIDENT PROPRIETORS.*

Shall not the phantom-axe, with viewless strokes,
The quiet purlieus of your traffic vex?
And the grim voice of all these aged oaks
Go storming o'er your ledgers, to perplex
Your clerks with sylvan horror? This fair haunt
Of light and shadow, and divine repose,
Low-fallen at last beneath your ruthless blows,
Waits its last shame, the hammer. Do not vaunt
The pelf your ravage brings you; for the ban
Of all the woods is on you! you have spared
No shelter for the dreams of god or man.
Who stirr'd the wood-god's bile, what risks he ran
Of old! ay, even the heedless swain, who dared
To tune his pipe across the nose of Pan!

CCXXIV.

THE NEEDLES' LIGHTHOUSE FROM KEYHAVEN, HAMPSHIRE.

The downs and tender-tinted cliffs are lost,
And nothing but the guardian fire remains—
That crimson-headed tower on the rough coast,
Whose steady lustre ceases not, nor wanes,
Till sunrise from the east reveals to us
The mighty Vectian wold, and tawny tract
Of shingle, seen through bowers of arbutus,
Like some fair corn-field, mellow and compact.
How that deep glow the deepening gloom attests !
How much is by that noble lighthouse taught !
Mine eye rests on it, as the spirit rests
In sorrow, on some holy, ardent thought,
The sole beam in our darkness !   Those who dwell
Near these great beacons are instructed well.

CCXXV.

DANGER—A PERSONIFICATION.

Grim Danger left his home in chartless wastes
To count his chances in our narrow seas ;
What anchors he might drag, what noble masts
Disable, on the rock or in the breeze :
And while he rode the waves from place to place
Like Hermes, his rude eyes the lighthouse met ;
And, as it seem'd to scan his heathen face
At leisure, he was dazzled and beset.
Morn dawn'd—in haste he bade the winds prepare
To wreck at eve the outgoing fisherman :
But Fitzroy heard—the storm-drum rose in air,
And not a coble but had changed its plan ;
While in his ears the spit-buoys swung their bells
He could not dodge our English sentinels.

CCXXVI.

A FAREWELL TO THE ISLE OF WIGHT.

Silent I gazed upon our foaming wake,
And silent on the Island hills I gazed,
As up the ebbing stream we bore, to make
Our harbour, while the West athwart us blazed.
Keen were my thoughts : my memory wander'd back
To those fair shores—the Needles and the Downs—
The happy woodlands and the little towns—
For every day a new and pleasant track ;
How grieved was I those social walks to lose,
Those friendly hands ! The shadow of our mast
And sail ran sadly o'er the fruitless ooze
At sunset, as between the banks we pass'd
Of that tide-fallen river, speeding fast
To land, and further from those fond adieus.

CCXXVII.

THE WHITE HORSE OF WESTBURY.

As from the Dorset shore I travell'd home,
I saw the charger of the Wiltshire wold ;
A far-seen figure, stately to behold,
Whose groom the shepherd is, the hoe his comb ;
His wizard-spell even sober daylight own'd ;
That night I dream'd him into living will ;
He neigh'd—and, straight, the chalk pour'd down
    the hill ;
He shook himself, and all beneath was stoned ;
Hengist and Horsa shouted o'er my sleep,
Like fierce Achilles ; while that storm-blanch'd horse
Sprang to the van of all the Saxon force,
And push'd the Britons to the Western deep ;
Then, dream-wise, as it were a thing of course,
He floated upwards, and regain'd the steep.

CCXXVIII.

BEAU NASH.

'Alas, alas!' said Moschus in his woe,
When Bion died, 'he comes not back to sing
His songs, nor other lip his notes can bring
From the same pipe.' So Bath regrets her Beau :
Her waters bubble upward without stop,
Each market sees her flowers and fruits replaced ;
Potherbs and roses—plums of every taste—
And peaches, brimming with ambrosial slop ;
All this repeats itself, a constant birth ;
But mighty Nash, strong-will'd and bold and shrewd,
Who awed and charm'd that modish multitude,
Hath found no heirs, and to the hollow earth
Bequeaths his fame ; for none his place may take ;—
Long have such honours slept, and may not reawake !

CCXXIX.

A PHOTOGRAPH ON THE RED GOLD.

Jersey, 1867.

About the knoll the airs blew fresh and brisk,
And, musing as I sat, I held my watch
Upon my open palm ; its smooth bright disk
Was uppermost, and so it came to catch,
And dwarf, the figure of a waving tree,
Back'd by the West.   A tiny sunshine peep'd
About a tiny elm,—and both were steep'd
In royal metal, flaming ruddily :
How lovely was that vision to behold !
How passing sweet that fairy miniature,
That stream'd and flicker'd o'er the burning gold !
God of small things and great ! do Thou ensure
Thy gift of sight, till all my days are told,
Bless all its bliss, and keep its pleasures pure !

CCXXX.

ON BOARD A JERSEY STEAMER.

A Midsummer Sunrise.

Long had I watch'd, and, summon'd by the ray
From those small window-lights, that dipt and bow'd
Down to the glimpsing waters, made my way
On deck, while the sun rose without a cloud ;
The brazen plates upon the steerage-wheel
Flash'd forth ; the steersman's face came full in view ;
Found at his post, he met the bright appeal
Of morning-tide, and answer'd ' I am true ! '
Then back again into my berth I crept,
And lay awhile, at gaze, with upward eye,
Where gleams and shadows from the ocean swept,
And flicker'd wildly o'er the dreaming fly,
That clung to the low ceiling.   Then I slept
And woke, and sought once more the sea and sky.

CCXXXI.

VIE DE JÉSUS.

On hearing of a forthcoming cheap edition.

A book of pleasant phrase, but narrow span
Of thought, is coming, in its cheapest guise,
Home to the hearths of each poor artisan
Throughout unhappy France—to make him wise
With a false gospel ; and that, so enticed,
And flush'd with petty raptures, he may give
His horny hands to this Parisian Christ,
Who lacks the strength to lift them ! Shall it live
This pleasant book ? Oh ! join with one accord !
Reject the lore, which—void of spleen or joke,
And in wild earnest—cuts down at one stroke
The measure of the stature of our Lord,
To this unscriptural pigmy ! nor invoke
A frail young saint, in lieu of God the Word !

CCXXXII.

POOR HODGE AND THE REV. SANS FOY.

Christmas.

Poor Hodge prays hard—the wise man smiles em-
    bower'd ;
The priest-philosopher, who lurks within
That screen of Christmas hollies, though empower'd
For other ends, takes pay for conscious sin :
What does the white-robed hireling, simpering thus
At his poor neighbour's spiritual desire?
Of all that honest faith incredulous,
The tainted vestal mocks the holy fire !
He lives beneath that little twinkling creed
Which counts for light at Tübingen ; his list
Of Christian sympathies is brief indeed :
And yet he speaks right loyally for Christ !
Ah ! traitorous lips ! so Judas falsely kiss'd
The Truth, with thirty pieces for his meed.

CCXXXIII.

PRAY, THINK, AND STRIVE!

Wouldst thou be safe from those, who plead or sneer
Against the virtue of our ancient frame
Of thought, and noble models ; wouldst thou claim
A full exemption from this modern Fear,
Pray, think, and strive ! with God's good Book for
    guide :
Be proof against the sweet word or the scoff :
A light-laid faith will soon be lifted off
Into some scorner's nostrils, when his pride
Smells at your simple creed in free disdain ;
Nor let the smile of gentler critics fix
Their spells upon you—they who deftly mix
Some Christian truth with errors black as Styx ;
Charming to sleep the conscience and the brain,
Without the spleen of coarser heretics.

*The following Sonnets, as far as No. CCXCII.,
were published in* 1873 *and dedicated to Agnes Grace
Weld :—*

CCXXXIV.

LITTLE SOPHY BY THE SEASIDE.

Young Sophy leads a life without alloy
Of pain ; she dances in the stormy air ;
While her pink sash and length of golden hair
With answering motion time her step of joy !
Now turns she through that seaward gate of heaven,
That opens on the sward above the cliff,—
Glancing a moment at each barque and skiff,
Along the roughening waters homeward driven ;
Shoreward she hies, her wooden spade in hand,
Straight down to childhood's ancient field of play,
To claim her right of common in the land
Where little edgeless tools make easy way—
A right no cruel Act shall e'er gainsay,
No greed dispute the freedom of the sand.

CCXXXV.

THE BUTTERFLY AND THE ROSE.

She pluck'd a wild wood-rose, and fondly strove,
With pausing step and ever-anxious care,
To carry home her dainty treasure-trove,
A butterfly, perch'd on those petals fair ;
Soon the gay creature flutter'd off again ;
And then her girlish fingers dropp'd the flower :
Ah ! little maid, when Love asserts his power,
This lesson, duly learnt, may save thee pain ;
Why from the forest-rose thine hand unclasp,
Because the fickle insect would not stay?
Not all the tendance of thy sweet blue eye,
And tiptoe heed, secured the butterfly ;
The flower, that needed but thy gentle grasp
To hold it, thou hast lightly thrown away !

CCXXXVI.

NAUSICAA.

Oft, from my classic memory's inmost shade,
That fair Phæacian shore to light I bring,
Where young Nausicaa stood,—that royal maid,
Whose brave-eyed pity faced the naked king,
And made a shipwreck sweet.   Beside the bed
Of a near stream he found the robe and oil,
Her timely present to the man of toil ;
Anon she took the chariot-reins, and led
The way, while in among her train he pass'd :
Then to the sacred grove, when they had come
Near that unsocial city ; till, at last,
He hail'd his sea-star in her own bright home,—
The girl who clothed his shame, and by the clue
Of purple yarn, foreshow'd him where to sue.

CCXXXVII.

THE DYING SCULPTOR.

'I hear my comrades' tools at busy morn,'
The youthful sculptor said ; 'but my poor name
Must die, like some poor babe that dies unborn,
While they may follow Phidias in his fame ;
I may not lift my head above the crowd ;
My marble visions are dissolving fast ;
My dream of art flits like some snow-white cloud
From weary eyes, that watch it to the last,
Before they sleep ; and thou, my last design !
Wherein I fondly hoped would reappear
The model glories of the Belvidere,
With his proud-postured grace in every line ;
'Tis time I learn'd, while slowly fading here,
To study lowlier attitudes than thine.'

CCXXXVIII.

FREE GREECE.

An Aspiration on the Accession of Prince George of Denmark.

Now are we free to range thee, hill and plain,
O Greece ! for thou thyself art also free ;
To muse at Athens, near the Maiden's fane,
Or land on Argos from the morning sea,
And spread our sails about thee lovingly : [1]
What joy thy pupils of the West shall feel
To dream the old war-notes, or the softer peal
Of pastoral sound from folds of Arcady !
Whence oft the gadding Faunus, tired of home,
In later times went off in sudden haste
From old Lycæus to fair Lucretil, [2]
To fend the Sabine farm from sun or blast,
And lent himself to that sweet lyric will,
Which led the Gods and Muses off to Rome.

---

[1] ' Singula dum capti circumvectamur amore.'
VIRGIL'S Georgics.

[2] ' Velox amœnum sæpe Lucretilem
Mutat Lycæo Faunus et igneam
Defendit æstatem capellis
Usque meis, pluviosque ventos.
HORACE, Od. I. 17.

T

CCXXXIX.

THE SEASIDE,

In and out of the Season.

In summer-time it was a paradise
Of mountain, frith, and bay, and shining sand;
Our outward rowers sang towards the land,
Follow'd by waving hands and happy cries:
By the full flood the groups no longer roam;
And when, at ebb, the glistening beach grows wide,
No barefoot children race into the foam,
But passive jellies wait the turn of tide.
Like some forsaken lover, lingering there,
The boatman stands; the maidens trip no more
With loosen'd locks; far from the billows' roar
The Mauds and Maries knot their tresses fair,
Where not a foam-flake from th' enamour'd shore
Comes down the sea-wind on the golden hair.

CCXL.

THE BARMOUTH SEA-BRIDGE.

When the train cross'd the sea, 'mid shouts of joy,
And the huge sea-pillars dash'd away the tide,
Awhile the power of song seem'd vague, beside
Those vast mechanics, mighty to convoy
A length of cars high over flood and ooze;
But the brief thought was feeble and unwise:
No season'd oak is stronger than the Muse,
For all the great cross-beams, and clamps, and ties.
Brave songs may raise a people sore-deprest,
And knit its strength together for the strife
With foreign foes, or subtle statesman's art:
Sweet hymns have lifted many a dying heart
Above the world, and sped the passing life
Across the waters, to the land of rest!

CCXLI.

ON A CHILD'S EYES.

How loveable all infant beauties are !
How sweet, in form and colour, are thine eyes !
Disks of two living flowers, that, rooted far
Within thy spirit, do report its joys,
And pass its half-hour's sorrows on to heaven,
To sun themselves and vanish ; but, in prayer,
Their best expression comes ; through the deep air
They see their Lord, like those of holy Stephen.
Far off, dear child ! be that unhappy time,
When aught of hard or shrewd shall settle there,
Of wanton boldness, or of blighting crime ;
So Age may haply find them, as they were,
And Death assort them with full many a one,
That shall not blench when Jesus takes His throne !

CCXLII.

LITTLE NORA,

Or the Portrait.

I ask'd of little Nora, but he gave
A piteous sigh—his answer did not come ;
My friend stood gazing on his daughter's tomb,
Till, with a sudden shame, I saw it too ;
At last he said : ' She died three moons ago :'
So long entomb'd had little Nora been,
So long I knew not of her father's woe !
Then came her portrait forth, which I had seen,
And he had shown with pride, when last we met ;
The same bright smile—the rose-o'erladen arms,
And all her pretty sum of infant-charms ;
But lo ! a fair memorial tress was set,
Facing the porcelain picture. where his child
Still nursed her pile of summer-wreaths and smiled.

CCXLIII.

OUR MARY AND THE CHILD-MUMMY.

When the four quarters of the world shall rise,
Men, women, children, at the Judgment-time,
Perchance this Memphian girl, dead ere her prime,
Shall drop her mask, and with dark new-born eyes
Salute our English Mary, loved and lost;
The Father knows her little scroll of prayer,[1]
And life as pure as His Egyptian air;
For, though she knew not Jesus, nor the cost
At which He won the world, she learn'd to pray;
And though our own sweet babe on Christ's good name
Spent her last breath, premonish'd and advised
Of Him, and in His glorious Church baptized,
She will not spurn this old-world child away,
Nor put her poor embalmèd heart to shame.

---

[1] The extract from the 'Book of the Dead,' which was put into the hands of the deceased.

CCXLIV.

CALLED FROM BED,

Or Lizzie and Kate.

With merry eyes against the golden west,
Two baby girls half-sat, and half reposed ;
And prattled in the sunshine, ere they closed
That summer's eve in childhood's balmy rest ;
But, hark ! their mother calls them from below,
She bids them rise ! Right glad we were to see
The twain, whose happy talk came down the stee,[1]
Lizzie and Kate, with night-gear white as snow,
And winsome looks : And when, with nod and smile,
And kiss for each, we left the woodside cot,
Upon the warm bright threshold for awhile
They stood, as we look'd back upon the spot,
Where crimson hollyhocks made contrast sweet
With those white darlings, and their naked feet.

---

[1] Provincial for ladder.   Here it is the ladder up to the cottager's bedroom.

CCXLV.

EMMELINE.

She grows apace, thy darling Emmeline !
Her heart, erewhile but two feet from the ground,
Beats at a higher level, in the line
Of many archers, pressing daily round ;
She doffs aside the aim of Jones and Brown ;
But, though a surer arrow has been set
By a young marksman from the neighbouring town,
It lingers on the string,—he speaks not yet.
When two love well, events must onward move ;
She feels a winning hand is on the bow,
And, if he asks, she will not answer 'No ;'
And Emmeline to him is life's sole mark,
He knows she loves him, and she knows his love ;
Speed, gentle shaft ! thou aim'st not in the dark !

CCXLVI.

THE HYDRAULIC RAM,

Or, the Influence of Sound on Mood.

In the hall grounds, by evening-gloom conceal'd,
He heard the solitary water-ram
Beat sadly in the little wood-girt field,
So dear to both ! 'Ah ! wretched that I am !'
He said, 'and traitor to my love and her's !
Why did I vent those words of wrath and spleen,
That changed her cheek, and flush'd her gentle mien?
When will they yield her back, those jealous firs,
Into whose shelter two days since she fled
From my capricious anger, phantom-fed?
When will her sire his interdict unsay?
Or must I learn a lonely lot to bear,
As this imprison'd engine, night and day,
Plies its dull pulses in the darkness there?'

CCXLVII.

ON THE MONUMENT OF THE PRINCESS ELIZA-
BETH STUART IN NEWPORT CHURCH, ISLE
OF WIGHT.

Lo ! by our Queen's command, the Parian stone
Has brought to light a flower that shall not fade ;
As old-world seeds, up to the surface thrown,
Break in white blossom by the Sun's sweet aid,
And air their buried beauty ; so, at last,
This gentle, royal, persecuted maid
Has had her blameless memory upcast,
Like the white clover, long in darkness laid ;
How touchingly she died ! her languid head
Had fallen forward on her father's book,
The Martyr's dying present, ere he bled ;
But, on the last high morning, she shall look
Heavenwards, through Him whose precious blood was
    shed
For this long-hidden flower of Carisbrook.

CCXLVIII.

THE SICK ORPHAN,

Or the Couch in the open Air.

'Twas at the close of a warm summer's day,
We spread our orphan's couch in the sweet air ;
And she was happy as the healthiest there ;
While, with each changing posture, as she lay,
A star, that lurk'd within the whispering firs,
Look'd forth upon her, glistening tenderly ;
' How like,' she said, ' a mother's watchful eye,
' That wakes and brightens, when her infant stirs ! '
She loved God's world, that maiden meek and mild ;
She challenged kith and kin on every hand,
Like Francis of Assisi—that dear child
Spoke sisterly of flowers and song-birds wild ;
Till every listener lost his self-command,
And o'er her dying love-notes wept and smiled !

CCXLIX.

THE MISSING BRIDE.

The wedded girl exclaim'd, 'I'll hide, I'll hide !'
And so they sought her gaily far and near,
Till, first in wonder, then in mortal fear,
Hour after hour they look'd for the lost bride.
Oh ! would she peep from out the laurel-walk,
Or from yon pleachèd roses nod and smile,
We would forgive her all this mournful talk
And sad surmise, nor chide her girlish guile.
Years pass'd, long years ! when in an ancient chest,
Whose heavy lid had dropp'd upon its spring,
They found the object of a bygone quest,
A skeleton in bridal wreath and ring ;
And recognized, with hearts too full to speak,
The mystery of that fatal ' Hide and seek.'

CCL.

THE FIR-GROVE,

Or the fatal Flash.

Again the ripening crops begin to shine
Near the dark firs, where Agnes dropp'd and died,
Struck in a moment from her lover's side,
At that gay banquet, with its songs and wine ;
Well he remembers how the thunder broke
After the flash, that pierced their festal bower,
Where she lay prostrate in her hood and cloak,
Drawn round her, just to fend a summer-shower ;
Well he remembers, later in the year,
How, when the pine-grove rang with questing hounds,
His soul reverted to those social sounds,
Dear Friendship's voice, and Love's, more wildly dear,
And how the Hunt seem'd like a drunken brawl
Crossing the silence of a funeral.

CCLI.

Continued.

THE AXE FORBIDDEN.

That belt of pines is dearer to his heart,
Than all the busy interests of life;
Since, on that festal morn, he saw the dart
Of heaven descending on his plighted wife.
No axe comes there; the trees extend their shade;
His loving sorrow interdicts their fall,
And warns the woodman from the holy glade;
The death of Agnes has redeem'd them all!
Yon small white gate, deep-set in living green,
Through which she pass'd,—alas! without return,—
Though distant, oft in sunny gleams is seen;
Or when, before the rain, the sacred grove
Comes looming up, surcharged with death and love,
And bids the little gate stand forth and mourn!

CCLII.

ENGLAND'S HONOUR.

How easily the breath of God o'erwhelms
The nations that presume to live for gain !
And clogs the motion of imperial realms,
As our poor breath the fly upon the pane :
Though our deep-laden argosies rejoice
From port to port to drag the seething sea
Across the world, how helpless we may be
In one brief year, despite our trade and noise !
Too oft, when, burthen'd with our chests and bales,
From the four winds we bring our freightage home,
We help to strike our country's honour dumb ;
Her noble voice, once heard above the gales,
Is lost among the stowage, while the prayer
Of our weak neighbours finds us slow to dare

CCLIII.

Continued.

ENFORCED WAR.

What ! shall the wharf and warehouse block our view
Of truth and right ?   Shall we no help afford,
When petty states in their affliction sue,
Because our busy merchants flinch the sword?
What ! when redemption of our word is due,
Shall we make pretexts ?—shall no war be waged ?
The meekest saint would hold us disengaged
From thoughts of peace, to serve a cause so true :
When Nelson scour'd the ocean's vast expanse
In passionate haste, and, hugging every wind,
Rush'd to the East, his dodging foe to find,
And drove among the anchor'd ships of France
The yeast of his fierce voyage, the great strife
Was forced upon us,—yea, we fought for life !

CCLIV.

Continued.

DISHONOURABLE PEACE.

Our own and Europe's safety met in one ;
And so we sent our warriors to the field,
Or launch'd them on the deep, our arms to wield :
But ah ! when Christian honour pleads alone,
When nought is lost by abstinence from war,
And nought is urgent save a sister's prayer,
We shirk the purer mission, and prepare
To close our armouries with bolt and bar ;
We give into the callous hands of trade
Our living hearts—all martial help forbear—
For fear the stirring gun-smoke should invade
Our marts, or smutch our commerce here and there ;
We furl our flag, as shopmen in a trice
Roll up the web, that will not fetch a price.

CCLV.

ARMS OLD AND NEW.

How changed our warfare and the arms we wield
The Phalanx, once the Macedonian's pride,
Has fled dishearten'd from the battle-field,
Since Flamininus pierced its wounded side :
Gone is the Roman Legion's tramp and clang :
The Ram assaults not now the leaguer'd wall ;
Our English Bowman is beyond recall—
The Rifle cracks where late the arrow sang !
The Trumpet lingers yet beyond them all,
But to its voice no mail-clad warrior hies,
Nor lifts a shield against the cannon-ball ;
High up the Shrapnel holds its burning breath ;
Within our bays the grim Torpedo lies,—
We arm the depths above us and beneath !

CCLVI.

THE BOMB AND THE ORGAN.

An Incident of the Siege of Strasburg.

In the great Church the holy organ stood,
And took in all its lauds a glorious part,
Affecting every listener's ear and heart
With its own plaintive or ecstatic mood.
O thunderbolt of war ! what did'st thou there ?
Methinks, it suited with thy function more,
To burst the war-drum, or explode the store,
Or spurn their eagles into drift, than bear
Down on this ark of praise with hostile force :
They knew not, when they sped thee on thy course,
That thou would'st jar with sweet Saint Cecily
And their own Handel, swooping from the sky
To storm the organ with one crashing blow,
As though it were a fortress of the foe !

CCLVII.

TO A FRENCH POET AND REFUGEE.

The time is past—that time of little cheer,
When all the hedgerows ran in naked lines;
And all the leafless landscape, far and near,
Seem'd a rough sketch, to foil the celandines;
'Tis morn—'tis May! arouse thy drooping powers,
Sing of the bright June-roses ere they come,
Anticipate the Summer's blowing flowers,
Till thy sweet words seem bursting into bloom;
Dear poet-exile! greet the year's advance!
Yield not to grief, but with a hymn of praise
Salute the season and these cloudless days;
And, when the sunset shall constrain thy gaze,
Then, with the closing flowers and setting rays,
Bemoan the sorrows and defeats of France.

CCLVIII.

THE ASCENT OF SNOWDON.

How merrily they plied the Alpine staff
In climbing from the lowland farms and barns !
Upward and onward still, intent to quaff
The topmost airs, beyond the dark-blue tarns,
And silver mists and echoes ! how the gales
Of Snowdon braced the heart our Willie lost
Among the wild sweet faces of the vales !
How his cheek glow'd, and how his hair was tost !
While one poor wight, too weak for that steep track,
Sat with the boulders, and the shining threads
Of mountain-spiders, till his friends came back ;
And watch'd their light among the breezy ferns,
Their shy escapes and beautiful returns,
And caught and kiss'd the wandering thistle-seeds.

CCLIX.

THE CATTLE TRAIN.

Penmaenmawr.

All light or transient gloom—no hint of storm—
White wreaths of foam, born in blue waters, broke
Among the mountain shadows ; all bespoke
A summer's day on Mona and the Orme.
My open window overlook'd the rails,
When, suddenly, a cattle-train went by,
Rapt, in a moment, from my pitying eye,
As from their lowing mates in Irish vales ;
Close-pack'd and mute they stood, as close as bees,
Bewilder'd with their fright and narrow room ;
'Twas sad to see that meek-eyed hecatomb,
So fiercely hurried past our summer seas,
Our happy bathers, and our fresh sea-breeze,
And hills of blooming heather, to their doom.

CCLX.

Continued.

HUMAN SORROWS.

Our happy bathers,—pardon my romance !
I thought of gladness only, for the tide
Ran sparkling to the land in merry dance ;
But, oh ! what sorrows haunt our sweet seaside !
Man, child, and woman mourn the wide world o'er ;
Yon maiden's snowy foot, that meets the wave,
Has just come faltering from her lover's grave,
Just pass'd that orphan-group upon the shore ;
The yacht glides gaily on, but as it nears
The beach, I see a night-black dress on board ;
The lonely widow dreams of those three years
Of summer-voyaging with her lost lord :
Too oft, when human figures fill the scene,
We count from woe to woe, with no glad hearts
    between !

CCLXI.

THE ARTIST ON PENMAENMAWR.

That first September day was blue and warm,
Flushing the shaly flanks of Penmaenmawr;
While youths and maidens, in the lucid calm
Exulting, bathed or bask'd from hour to hour;
What colour-passion did the artist feel!
While evermore the jarring trains went by,
Now, as for evermore, in fancy's eye,
Smutch'd with the cruel fires of Abergele ; [1]
Then fell the dark o'er the great crags and downs,
And all the night-struck mountain seem'd to say,
'Farewell ! these happy skies, this peerless day !
And these fair seas—and, fairer still than they,
The white-arm'd girls in dark blue bathing-gowns,
Among the snowy gulls and summer spray.'

---

[1] English pronunciation.

CCLXII.

CADER IDRIS AT SUNSET.

Last autumn, as we sat, ere fall of night,
Over against old Cader's rugged face,
We mark'd the sunset from its secret place
Salute him with a fair and sudden light.
Flame-hued he rose, and vast, without a speck
Of life upon his flush'd and lonely side ;
A double rainbow o'er him bent, to deck
What was so bright before, thrice glorified !
How oft, when pacing o'er those inland plains,
I see that rosy rock of Northern Wales
Come up before me ! then its lustre wanes,
And all the frith and intermediate vales
Are darken'd, while our little group remains
Half-glad, half-tearful, as the vision pales !

CCLXIII.

THE OLD HILLS'-MAN AND HIS TRUCK.

How oft I met the old hills'-man and his truck,
Gleaning the refuse of that mountain-road !
How oft he stopp'd to chat and bless his luck,
Or talk how much to Providence he owed !
Fresh was his fancy, and his heart was full ;
His long-plied shovel had its own romance
For him, and every varying circumstance
Of earth and sky forbad him to be dull :
How oft he fish'd his treasure from the crest
Of rain-fed gullies, hurrying to the west
In the wild sunshine, when the storm went by,
Or came on earlier fortunes, in the eye
Of rosy morn, the roadster's first supply ;
Gay at all hours, and ever on the quest !

CCLXIV.

WELSH LUCY,

Or, the Duke of Monmouth's Mother.

Poor Lucy Walters ! who remembers thee?
Thy name is lost, though on thy native hill
Perchance they know it, yea, and see thee still
But, in the outer world, how few there be
To speak of Monmouth's mother !   To thy door
The tempter came, and thy young heart beguiled ;
Then came the birth of that half-royal child,
Who, when his feeble battle-shout was o'er,
Crept into lone Shag's Heath from lost Sedgemoor ;
Then fell his kinsman's axe, whose triple blow
Thy spirit still hears ! sore penance for that tryst
Of shame, which brought thy motherhood of woe—
Or sighs, at breaking of the mountain-mist,
To view each morn, the headsman's world below.

CCLXV.

THE LITTLE HEIR OF SHAME.

He was a little heir of shame—his birth
Announced by peevish voices, and his death
Welcomed by all; he staid not long on earth,
Nor vex'd them long with his fast-fleeting breath;
He felt their blows, too young to feel their scorn;
How that poor babe was beaten and reviled,
Because, albeit so mischievously born,
He wail'd as loudly as a lawful child!
They hurried to the goal his faltering pace;
Full soon they bore him to his mother's grave;
No more for other's sin accounted base,
In Paradise he shows his harmless face;
The Saviour flinches not from his embrace,
But gives him all his infant-heart can crave.

CCLXVI.

THE HARVEST MOON.

How peacefully the broad and golden moon
Comes up to gaze upon the reaper's toil !
That they who own the land for many a mile,
May bless her beams, and they who take the boon
Of scatter'd ears ; Oh ! beautiful ! how soon
The dusk is turn'd to silver without soil,
Which makes the fair sheaves fairer than at noon,
And guides the gleaner to his slender spoil ;
So, to our souls, the Lord of love and might
Sends harvest-hours, when daylight disappears ;
When age and sorrow, like a coming night,
Darken our field of work with doubts and fears,
He times the presence of His heavenly light
To rise up softly o'er our silver hairs.

CCLXVII.

OLD RURALITIES.

A Regret.

With joy all relics of the past I hail ;
The heath-bell, lingering in our cultured moor,
Or the dull sound of the slip-shoulder'd flail,
Still busy on the poor man's threshing-floor :
I love this unshorn hedgerow, which survives
Its stunted neighbours, in this farming age :
The thatch and house-leek, where old Alice lives
With her old herbal, trusting every page ;
I love the spinning-wheel, which hums far down
In yon lone valley, though, from day to day,
The boom of Science shakes it from the town.
Ah ! sweet old world ! thou speedest fast away !
My boyhood's world ! but all last looks are dear ;
More touching is the death-bed than the bier !

CCLXVIII.

TO A RED-WHEAT FIELD.

O rich red wheat ! thou wilt not long defer
Thy beauty, though thou art not wholly grown ;
The fair blue distance and the moorland fir
Long for thy golden laughter !   Four years gone,
How oft ! with eager foot, I scaled the top
Of this long rise, to give mine eye full range ;
And, now again, rotation brings the change
From seeds and clover, to my favourite crop ;
How oft I've watch'd thee from my garden, charm'd
With thy noon-stillness, or thy morning tears !
Or, when the wind clove and the sunset warm'd
Thine amber-shafted depths and russet ears ;
O ! all ye cool green stems ! improve the time,
Fulfil your beauty ! justify my rhyme !

CCLXIX.

TO A SCARECROW, OR MALKIN, LEFT LONG AFTER HARVEST.

Poor malkin, why hast thou been left behind?
The wains long since have carted off the sheaves,
And keen October, with his whistling wind,
Snaps all the footstalks of the crisping leaves;
Methinks thou art not wholly make-believe ;
Thy posture, hat, and coat, are human still ;
Could'st thou but push a hand from out thy sleeve !
Or smile on me ! but ah ! thy face is nil !
The stubbles darken round thee, lonely one !
And man has left thee, all this dreary term,
No mate beside thee—far from social joy ;
As some poor clerk survives his ruin'd firm,
And, in a napless hat, without employ,
Stands, in the autumn of his life, alone.

CCLXX.

THE WILLOW,

Or, the Rose-prop.

How shall I hew thee down, thou mighty bower?
My summer-tent, my waving canopy?
I love too well thy lithe submissive power,
Thy silver beauty is too dear to me;
At first, thou wert a little rose's prop,
A new-cut willow wand, that did'st o'erbear
Thy tiny nursling-plant; we took no care
To check thee, nor thy lavish growth to lop,
For thou art fair as any flower that blows;
But though thou art so pleasant to mine eye,
Methinks, each child of earth some sorrow knows,
Akin to ours; long since that infant rose
Droop'd ere its time, and bow'd its head to die,
While thou hast soar'd aloft, to toss and sigh!

X

CCLXXI.

THE OLD FOX-HUNTER.

To some this rich and multifarious world
Is void without the chase : poor Reynard's scent
Is the prime smell beneath the firmament,
And all besides is into Limbo hurl'd ;
To-day will be the first meet of the hounds ;
The wind blows south, and, in the early dark,
The squire sits gazing o'er his dusky park,
While, in his ears, the horn already sounds ;
Yon furzy levels harbour all his hopes,
No other field of glory ranks with them ;
Fair Athens and divine Jerusalem
Are moving to the Dawn with Hunter's Copse,
And the Home-cover ; but the squire ignores
All fame, that mounts not at his kennel-doors.

CCLXXII.

TO THE GOSSAMER-LIGHT.

Quick gleam ! that ridest on the gossamer !
How oft I see thee, with thy wavering lance,
Tilt at the midges in their evening dance,
A gentle joust set on by summer air !
How oft I watch thee from my garden-chair !
And, failing that, I search the lawns and bowers,
To find thee floating o'er the fruits and flowers,
And doing thy sweet work in silence there :
Thou art the poet's darling, ever sought
In the fair garden or the breezy mead ;
The wind dismounts thee not ; thy buoyant thread
Is as the sonnet, poising one bright thought,
That moves but does not vanish ! borne along
Like light,—a golden drift through all the song !

CCLXXIII.

ON FINDING A SMALL FLY CRUSHED IN A BOOK.

Some hand, that never meant to do thee hurt,
Has crush'd thee here between these pages pent;
But thou hast left thine own fair monument,
Thy wings gleam out and tell me what thou wert:
Oh! that the memories, which survive us here,
Were half as lovely as these wings of thine!
Pure relics of a blameless life, that shine
Now thou art gone.   Our doom is ever near:
The peril is beside us day by day;
The book will close upon us, it may be,
Just as we lift ourselves to soar away
Upon the summer-airs.   But, unlike thee,
The closing book may stop our vital breath,
Yet leave no lustre on our page of death.

CCLXXIV.

THE EAGLE AND THE SONNET.

As on the sceptre of the Olympian King
The Royal eagle sat, bedrowsed and still,
The Theban[1] sketch'd him, while the savage will
And strength of the great bird were slumbering ;
If Pindar drew him best with drooping wings,
And on a quiet perch his likeness took,
How shall the sonnet, least of rhythmic things,
Presume to take him flying ?   Will he brook
To wheel and hover, while I hunt for rhymes ?
Returning at the Muse's fitful times,
For yet another study ?   And, if so,
Will he not yearn at last to strike one blow
At his own miniature, and swoop from high
To clutch my climax with an angry cry ?

---

[1] " ἐν σκάπτῳ Διὸς —
—Ύγρὸν νῶτον αἰωρεῖ."
PINDAR.

CCLXXV.

GOUT AND WINGS.

The pigeons flutter'd fieldward, one and all,
I saw the swallows wheel, and soar, and dive;
The little bees hung poised before the hive,
Even Partlet hoised herself across the wall:
I felt my earth-bound lot in every limb,
And, in my envious mood, I half-rebell'd;
When lo! an insect cross'd the page I held,
A little helpless minim, slight and slim;
Ah! sure, there was no room for envy there,
But gracious aid and condescending care;
Alas! my pride and pity were misspent,
The atom knew his strength, and rose in air!
My gout came tingling back, as oft he went,
A wing was open'd at me everywhere!

CCLXXVI.

Continued.

PODAGER BEGS PARDON OF BIRDS, BEES, AND WINGS IN GENERAL.

Pardon me, all ye birds that float at ease,
That I begrudged your fleet aërial joys ;
And thou, poor Partlet ! and ye little bees,
That hum and hover with a pleasant noise
About your homes of honey ! 'twas a spirt
Of spleen—a peevish murmur of disease,
And not a measured curse to do you hurt :
And thou ! who for a moment did'st displease,
Commission'd to rebuke my pride, and spring
Thy tiny pennons on me unaware ;
Thy smart and sudden lesson was the thing
I needed.—Thou art gone I know not where !
But I have seen, beside my gouty chair,
A chiding angel, of the smallest wing.

CCLXXVII.

A COLONY OF NIGHTINGALES.

I placed the mute eggs of the Nightingale
In the warm nest, beneath a brooding thrush;
And waited long, to catch the earliest gush
Of the new wood-notes, in our northern vale;
And, as with eye and ear I push'd my search,
Their sudden music came as sweet to me,
As the first organ-tone to Holy Church,
Fresh from the Angel and St. Cecily;
And, year by year, the warblers still return
From the far south, and bring us back their song,
Chanting their joy our summer groves among,
A tune the merle and goldfinch cannot learn;
While the poor thrush, that hatch'd them, listens near,
Nor knows the rival choir she settled here!

CCLXXVIII.

THE SPARROW AND THE DEW-DROP.

When to the birds their morning meal I threw,
Beside one perky candidate for bread
There flash'd and wink'd a tiny drop of dew,
But while I gazed, I lost them, both had fled ;
His careless tread had struck the blade-hung tear,
And all its silent beauty fell away ;
And left, sole relic of the twinkling sphere,
A sparrow's dabbled foot upon a spray ;
Bold bird ! that didst efface a lovely thing
Before a poet's eyes ! I've half a mind,
Could I but single thee from out thy kind,
To mulct thee in a crumb ; a crumb to thee
Is not more sweet than that fair drop to me ;
Fie on thy little foot and thrumming wing !

CCLXXIX.

TO A CUCKOO IN A HIGHWAY HEDGE.

O cuckoo ! am I of my wits bereft ?
Or do I hear thee in the hedgerow there ?
The doves of old Dodona never left
Their oak, to babble near a thoroughfare ;
How shall thy mythic character outlive
Thy presence, by thy voice identified ?
How shall the fells and copses e'er forgive
Thy gadding visit to the highway-side ?
How art thou disenchanted ! self-betray'd !
Back, foolish bird ! return whence thou hast stray'd ;
A woody distance is thy vantage-ground ;
Thy song comes sweetest up from Moreham wood ;
Why notify thy claim to flesh and blood ?
The Muses know thee as a mystic sound.

CCLXXX.

THE SWAN AND THE PEACOCK.

Proud of his hundred eyes of glossy grain,
That watch'd in Argus once, but now are set
Firm in the streamers of his ample train,
The Peacock walks beside his lowlier mate ;
Or stands apart, unfolding all his state !
While, on the surface of yon glassy lake,
A snow-white swan, with sinuous neck elate,
Ruffles his shifting plumes for beauty's sake ;
One seems like some fair barge, the choice design
Of spotless fancies, for a maiden's joy,
To fare on summer-waters, when they shine ;
While the other, swimming in his majesty,
Though on firm ground, that eastern bark might be,
On Cydnus rigg'd to meet Mark Antony.

CCLXXXI.

MY TIMEPIECE.

The hour has struck its advent and farewell,
And hark ! another hour begins to beat !
As when a crier stops, and rings his bell
To tell a loss, then on with busy feet
To raise the cry elsewhere ; our flying hours
We waste, and baulk them of their noblest use ;
And so disable our best gifts and powers,
Or leave them open to the fiend's abuse ;
Or should I—the same moral to convey—
A more derisive apologue subjoin,
My clock's a mocking thief, who steals my coin,
Then, counting up the sum, as if to say,
' How many precious pieces I purloin,
One, two, three, four,'—trips daintily away.

CCLXXXII.

OUR NEW CHURCH.

As yet no organ rolls—no prayer-bell rings—
But in and out the darting swallows pass ;
While distant hands prepare the pictured glass,
Through vacant quatrefoils the hodman sings ;
But, when the House is built, the Table spread,
Enter, O! broken heart! and tell thy sin!
Prime guest of Jesus, enter! and begin
The Church's mystic life—one Cup, one Bread ;
As to these stone-heap'd graves the spring shall give,
Once more, their common bond of daisies sweet,
So may all crush'd and barren souls revive,
In one white field of common graces meet,
And bells, and organ, and glad hymns, combine
To draw them lovingly to rites divine!

CCLXXXIII.

OUR NEW CHURCH CLOCK.

Henceforward shall our Time be plainly read—
Down in the nave I catch the twofold beat
Of those full-weighted moments overhead ;
And hark ! the hour goes clanging down the street
To the open plain !　How sweet at eventide
Will that clear music be to toil-worn men !
Calling them home, each to his own fire-side ;
How sweet the toll of all the hours till then !
The cattle, too, the self-same sound shall hear,
But they can never know the power it wields
O'er human hearts, that labour, hope, and fear ;
Our village-clock means nought to steed or steer ;
The call of Time will share each twinkling ear
With summer flies and voices from the fields !

CCLXXXIV.

TWELVE O'CLOCK AT NOON.

The sound of noon floats o'er the village-pool,
Round the babe's cradle and the blind man's chair,
And far afield ; each buffet on the air
Is whisper'd back by wandering hearts at school,
The sweetest sum they do !   Our Time has got
A presence and a motion, and looks forth
On all, and speaks to all—misprized or not ;
What earthly language has a holier worth ?
And though my little watch reports to me
The measure of my life more tenderly
Than these great seconds, with their iron gear,
That serve the booming hours—I love to hear
That fair and open reckoning, night and day,
Which tells us boldly how we pass away !

CCLXXXV.

THE AFTERNOTE OF THE HOUR.

The hour had struck, but still the air was fill'd
With the long sequence of that mighty tone ;
A wild Æolian afternote, that thrill'd
My spirit, as I kiss'd that dear headstone ;
A voice that seem'd through all the Past to go—
From the bell's mouth the lonely cadence swept,
Like the faint cry of unassisted woe,
Till, in my profitless despair, I wept ;
My hope seem'd wreck'd ! but soon I ceased to mourn ;
A nobler meaning in that voice I found,
Whose scope lay far beyond that burial-ground ;
'Twas grief, but grief to distant glory bound !
Faith took the helm of that sweet wandering sound,
And turn'd it heavenwards, to its proper bourne.

CCLXXXVI.

AFTER THE SCHOOL-FEAST.

The Feast is o'er—the music and the stir—
The sound of bat and ball, the mimic gun ;
The lawn grows darker, and the setting sun
Has stolen the flash from off the gossamer,
And drawn the midges westward ; youth's glad cry—
The smaller children's fun-exacting claims,
Their merry raids across the graver games,
Their ever-crossing paths of restless joy,
Have ceased—And, ere a new Feast-day shall shine,
Perchance my soul to other worlds may pass ;
Another head in childhood's cause may plot,
Another Pastor muse in this same spot,
And the fresh dews, that gather on the grass
Next morn, may gleam in every track but mine !

Y

CCLXXXVII.

THE MURDER OF BISHOP PATTESON.

When far from home some noble martyr dies,
We read his sacred story o'er and o'er;
Like incense, drifting from a sacrifice,
His name blows sweet from that disastrous shore,
O'er the broad waters, to his native land;
But, though our martyr'd saint has fallen asleep,
And closed his ardent eyes, we need not weep;
Unfoil'd the purpose of the Lord shall stand!
His world-wide Church out-grows the powers of Hell,
His holy Ark expands!   O'er lands and seas
The golden wings of Cherubim shall meet,
Till all the tribes shall own one Mercy-seat:
The school of faithful prophets shall not cease
With him, who loved his hundred isles so well !

CCLXXXVIII.

THE PASTOR'S PRAYER.

At dawn, he marks the smoke among the trees,
From hearths, to which his daily footsteps go ;
And hopes and fears and ponders on his knees,
If his poor sheep will heed his voice or no ;
What wholesome turn will Ailsie's sorrow take?
Her latest sin will careless Annie rue ?
Will Robin now, at last, his wiles forsake ?
Meet his old dupes, yet hold his balance true ?
He prays at noon, with all the warmth of heaven
About his heart, that each may be forgiven ;
He prays at eve : and through the midnight air
Sends holy ventures to the throne above ;
His very dreams are faithful to his prayer,
And follow, with closed eyes, the path of love.

CCLXXXIX.

TO THE HOLY VIRGIN.

Mother of Him who made us ! first of mothers !
Who heard'st the glorious angel bid thee 'Hail !'
Mother of Him who call'd mankind His brothers,
Although His dying rent the Temple's veil,
And utter darkness told He was divine ;
A few brief scriptures show us more of thee,
Than all these after-times of pageantry,
The marble statue, and the jewell'd shrine ;
The passionate acclaim of many lands
Has drown'd thine own sweet voice, that ever spake
Of the Lord's handmaid ; now they bid thee take
His place, and wrong thee with adoring hands ;
But oh ! we know thee best, when seen alone,
Far in the Past, with Jesus and with John !

CCXC.

THE PALM-WILLOW.

I read the Gospel-record of those cries
Of praise, that ran before the Friday's harm ;
Till late, on Palm-sun eve, I closed mine eyes,
Grasping the glossy spray we call a palm ;
I dream'd—a fond presumptuous pity took
My soul ; I seem'd to line the coming crown
Of thorns, with cushions of the silver down
From those cool sallows, cut beside the brook ;
But, on the act, quick came the reprimand,
'What mean'st thou, sinner ! with pretentious hand
To staunch the life-blood of the Incarnate Son ?
Without My wounds, the world remains undone ;
Why dost thou, then, forbid thy Lord to bleed ?
Why grudge mankind the Passion and the Creed ? '

CCXCI.

Continued.

A RECANTATION.

'Twas Christ that spoke, while sitting on the Ass
Beneath the brows of Olivet, He gazed
Upon the rebel city, which, alas !
Was, in His weeping eyes, already razed :
Calm'd by His mild rebuke, I could not chide
Nor wipe His tears, and though His utmost grief
Lay bare before me, proffer'd no relief,
But, 'Oh ! forgive my folly, Lord,' I cried,—
Vailing the fair presumptuous palm I bore,
To the dark Cross His meeker servant wore ;
' Or I would rather be this little foal
That stands and waits, where Thou would'st wait and
　　weep,
Than the light thinker, who would fain control
Thy love, and lull Thy holy pains to sleep.'

CCXCII.

ON SOME HUMMING-BIRDS IN A GLASS CASE.

For vacant song behold a shining theme !
These dumb-struck flutterers from Indian land,
The colour on whose crests, sweet Nature's hand,
Fulfils our richest thought of crimson gleam ;
Whose wings, thus spread and balanced forth, might
    seem
Slender as serpent's tongue or fairy's wand—
And, as with vantage of the sun we stand,
Each glossy bosom kindles in his beam ;
Ah me ! how soon does human death impair
The tender beauty of the fairest face,
Whatever balms and unguents we prepare !
While these resplendent creatures bear no trace,
Bright-bosom'd and bright-crested as they are,
No soil, nor token of the tomb's disgrace !

The remaining Sonnets are new : all but four or five, which have appeared in magazines.

CCXCIII.

LOCALITIES OF BURNS.

When the bright crescent gleam'd o'er hill and dale
We saw the poet's lowly place of birth,
The Kirk, erewhile the scene of fiendish mirth,
The brig that parted Maggie and her tail.
We saw his bust, we saw the cenotaph,
Which on the skirts of that fair garden stands,
And Tam o' Shanter with his soundless laugh
Over his empty cup and stony hands—
All these were present, but the bard was gone,
No more to tune his pipe on plain or hill,
Nor multiply the moon from Willie's mill.
But oh ! how fondly still that crescent moon·
Hung with her golden horns o'er bonnie Doon,
As though she look'd to be mis-counted still.

CCXCIV

TO A STARVED HARE IN THE GARDEN IN WINTER.

Soft-footed stroller from the herbless wood,
Stealing so mutely through my garden ground,
I will not balk thine eager quest for food,
Nor take thy life, nor startle thee with sound.
I spared the wanton squirrel, though I saw
His autumn raid upon my nuts and cones ;
I spared his frisky brush and bushy jaw ;
And shall I wound the poor dishearten'd ones?
Come freely : in my heart thy charter lies ;
Feed boldly—what thou gain'st I cannot lose.
When robin shuffles on the snow-white sill,
We serve his winsome hunger ; who would choose
To daunt his ruddy breast and wistful eyes?
But, hare or robin, it is hunger still.

CCXCV.

*ON THE SECULARISTS' NOTION OF MAKING OUR
CHURCHES INTO MUSEUMS AND EXHIBITIONS.*

What noble work our seculars can do !
Behold their church museum ; come and see
The mighty change, the change from false to true,
To sense and fact from idle mystery !
Apes, mummies, minerals are scatter'd o'er
The nave ; new wines and patents meet our eyes ;
Young prigs and gnostic maidens pace the floor ;
The altar's self is mask'd with butterflies.
Ah ! guileless symbols of ungodly scorn !
If your bright wings were still alive and free,
How would ye float and tremble silently
About the holy place, this blessed morn !
Alas ! our science is but shame and loss,
When pack'd and pinn'd to overlay the cross !

CCXCVI.

THE AIR REGISTER,

With reference to a speech of Henry VIII.'s, ' Let us go a-hunting,'
when Queen Anna's execution was accomplished.

When the Tower gun announced Queen Anna's death,
And straight the king proclaim'd a hunting day,
He dream'd not how that signal, and the breath
Of those brief words, would never fleet away.
He dream'd not how the booming of that gun
Would be a deathless pulse through space and time,
And his own royal voice be drifted on
With all its scorn.   The motion of a crime
Soon meets the sorrowing angels; but, if true
That nature has this sin-recording force,
Each nobler act and utterance takes its course
Through the same air, and is immortal too.
And every deed of love and breath of prayer
Shall make its own memorial current there.

CCXCVII.

AN EVENING IN HARVEST TIME.

On goes the age with footsteps fleet and strong,
And we have seen a wondrous sight to-day ;
The mighty Chariot-reaper forced its way
Where erst the half-hidden scythes-man stoop'd along.
Another tale of harvest hours is o'er,
With all its great, and all its little gains,
And poor old Ailsie piles her wheaten store,
And feels as rich as all the rolling wains.
The moonrise seems to burn a golden oil,
To light a world of plenty, while it shows
The woodland, listening in its dark repose
To many a voice and homeward step of toil,
Till all have pass'd beyond the forest bound,
And not a footfall chafes it into sound.

CCXCVIII.

NATURE AND LANGUAGE.

Oft, when some happy thought for song is found,
It flits about us like a living thing,
Returning, like the swallow, from each round,
With some new charm of light on breast and wing.
On such fair themes we lavish all our skill,
Though all our skill can scarce their grace record;
A residue of beauty lingers still,
Beyond our fondest art, or latest word.
How seldom does our choicest phrase fulfil
Our heart's desire, or reach our depths of will!
But, when we quit this life of day and hour,
With souls enfranchised, and with sins forgiven,
Our eloquence will be a readier power,
While all our sweetest thoughts go safe to heaven.

CCXCIX.

THE CLASSIC LARK.

Farewell, sweet bird, so winsome and so wise!
Though the blue heavens were native to thy flight,
My desk and papers seem'd thy prime delight,
Those odes, and epics, and anthologies!
Methinks, thou wert so fond of ancient lore,
A classic welcome in the shades below
Awaits thee, now thy learned life is o'er:
To fair Elysian meadows thou shalt go,
A happy region, void of rain and storm;
But when the Stygian boatman chirps to thee
Thy wings expand, thy buoyant heart rebels:
High over Styx I see thy twinkling form;
I hear old Charon shouting for his fee,
While thou art poised above the asphodels!

CCC.

*ON SEEING A LITTLE CHILD SPIN A COIN OF
ALEXANDER THE GREAT.*

This is the face of him, whose quick resource
Of eye and hand subdued Bucephalus,
And made the shadow of a startled horse
A foreground for his glory.   It is thus
They hand him down ; this coin of Philip's son
Recalls his life, his glories, and misdeeds ;
And that abortive court of Babylon,
Where the world's throne was left among the reeds.
His dust is lost among the ancient dead,
A coin his only presence : he is gone :
And all but this half mythic image fled—
A simple child may do him shame and slight ;
'Twixt thumb and finger take the golden head,
And spin the horns of Ammon out of sight.

CCCI.

TO A 'TENTING' BOY.

Early thou goest forth, to put to rout
The thievish rooks, that all about thee sail ;
While thy tin tube, and monitory shout
Report thy lonely function to the vale ;
From spot to spot thou rovest far and near,
While the sick ewe in the next pasture ground
Lifts her white eyelash, points her languid ear,
And turns her pensive face towards the sound ;
All day thy little trumpet wails about
The great brown field, and, whilst I slowly climb
The grassy slope, with ready watch drawn out,
To meet thy constant question of the time,
Methinks I owe thee much, my little boy,
For this new duty, and its quiet joy.

CCCII.

EAST OR WEST?

I sat within a window, looking west,
On a fair autumn eve; the forest leaves
Moved o'er a fiery sunset, vision blest
After that day of storm and rainy eaves.
While thus I gazed, I heard a sweet voice cry:—
'Come to the east, and see the rainbow die.
On the last shower anon the moon will rise,
And light the village when the rainbow dies.'
Betwixt the two I could not well decide;
For each was fair, and both would vanish soon.
But that sweet voice cried eastward still: I knew
No light would pierce the wood when day withdrew;
So I went east and to the rising moon
The village brighten'd when the rainbow died.

CCCIII.

THE FLOCK FOR THE MARKET:

Or, Hope and Despondency.

Two hundred strong they pour'd into the field,
A gentle host, for one brief night's repose
Before the market, for their doom was seal'd ;
They left their pasture ere the morn arose.
I listen'd, while that multitudinous sound
Peal'd from the highway through the twilight air,
A cry for light, while all was dark around,
A throng of voices like a people's prayer ;
Slow broke the dawn ; the flock went plodding on
Into the distance, some at once to bleed,
Some to be scatter'd wide on moor and mead.
But while I sigh'd to think that all were gone,
A little lark, their field-mate of the night,
Saw them from heaven and sang them out of sight.

CCCIV.

PAULUM SYLVÆ,

Or, a Plea for a Garden Grove.

Thou bid'st me take the axe, and rudely smite
Yon belt of trees that bounds thy searching eyes.
Thou hast a stranger's heart, an alien's sight,
For all those dear home objects which I prize ;
I love the rooks, that drop the wearied wing
At eve so fondly on their native grove,
And to mine ear and eyesight daily bring
So many sounds and motions that I love ;
And in that path beneath, ere day is done,
How oft I pace beside the setting sun ;
How oft I watch the nightly orb arise
On the dark trees, my garden guest to be.
I will not throw her back on open skies,
No axe shall part my woodland moon and me.

CCCV.

THE LECTERN'S FOOT,

Or Maud and Willie.

A little pile of gourd, and flower, and fruit,
As up the aisle I go, salutes mine eyes—
Our bright thanksgiving at the lectern's foot,
A sweet compendious mellow harvest lies :
But where are Maud and Willie, wont to be
Both in their place at seasons such as these ?
Alas, they perished in the chill March breeze,
Though still they seem alive and bright to me ;
Though many a month of sorrow intervenes,
Since last I heard their hymns and saw them pray,
I still recall the frosty winter gleam,
When, on the morn of their last Christmas day,
They stood, and sang beneath the moted beam
That cross'd the church, and pierced the evergreens.

CCCVI.

LETTY'S GLOBE.

When Letty had scarce pass'd her third glad year,
And her young, artless words began to flow,
One day we gave the child a colour'd sphere
Of the wide earth, that she might mark and know,
By tint and outline, all its sea and land.
She patted all the world; old empires peep'd
Between her baby fingers; her soft hand
Was welcome at all frontiers.   How she leap'd,
And laugh'd, and prattled in her world-wide bliss;
But when we turned her sweet unlearned eye
On our own isle, she raised a joyous cry,
'Oh! yes, I see it, Letty's home is there!'
And, while she hid all England with a kiss,
Bright over Europe fell her golden hair.

CCCVII.

THE OAK AND THE HILL.

When the storm fell'd our oak, and thou, fair wold,
Wast seen beyond it, we were slow to take
The lesson taught, for our old neighbour's sake.
We thought thy distant presence wan and cold,
And gave thee no warm welcome ; for, whene'er
We tried to dream him back into the place,
Where late he stood, the giant of his race,
'Twas but to lift an eye, and thou wert there,
His sad remembrancer, the monument
That told us he was gone ; but thou hast blent
Thy beauty with our loss so long and well,
That, in all future griefs, we may foretell
Some lurking good behind each seeming ill,
Beyond each fallen tree some fair blue hill.

CCCVIIL

THE MUTE LOVERS ON THE RAILWAY JOURNEY.

They bad farewell ; but neither spoke of love.
The railway bore him off with rapid pace,
He gazed awhile on Edith's garden grove,
Till alien woodlands overlapp'd the place—
Alas ! he cried, how mutely did we part !
I fear'd to test the truth I seem'd to see.
Oh ! that the love dream in her timid heart
Had sigh'd itself awake, and called for me !
I could have answer'd with a ready mouth,
And told a sweeter dream ; but each forebore.
He saw the hedgerows fleeting to the north
On either side, whilst he look'd sadly forth :
Then set himself to face the vacant south,
While fields and woods ran back to Edith More.

CCCIX.

A NIGHT-CHARGE AGAINST A SWAN BY A LOVER.

The swan, wild-clanging, scoured the midnight lake,
And broke my dream of Annie, and I lay,
Through those brief hours before the dawn of day,
Chiding the sound that startled me awake.
Ungracious bird, why didst thou come between
My loving question and her dear reply?
I saw her parted lip, her downcast eye,
I saw how sweet her answer would have been,
Hadst thou not cried just then in love's despite!
For once, I pray, thy clamorous zeal forbear,
And grant this easy boon to me and her:
I claim my perfect dream: be mute to-night:
Thy voice kept Annie silent: I foresee
Thy silence will be Annie's voice to me.

CCCX.

THE SEA-SIDE TRUANTS

Wildly she pass'd along that crowded shore,
With earnest eye fix'd on the ocean rim :
On came the tide, and all would soon wax dim,
And she might never see her darlings more.
But lo ! what means that sail-like line of light,
Advancing from the border of the sea
Into that stream of glory, golden-bright?
The mother's eye divines its mystery :
Ah ! yes, it is her little white-robed band
Of children wading in the sunny brine,
That winds about the hollows in the sand :
And now, too near for doubt, they glance and shine.
Her sight was true : that far off snowy line
Was Maud and Mary, Kate and Caroline.

CCCXI.

THE INNOCENT LISTENER.

The widow stood beside her husband dead :
He was a man of harsh and stubborn cast ;
Who hugg'd his selfish vices to the last,
And scoff 'd at faith, even on his dying bed.
I spoke of love, and faith, and holy fear,
And all a patient heart could bear and do :
The mother listen'd with attentive ear,
And the poor infant seem'd to listen too.
She stretch'd her arms towards the psalm and prayer,
Forward she lean'd, as if in earnest heed,
And on the wond'rous sound attentive hung :
What sweet and wistful innocence was there,
Her open mouth and little wordless tongue,
Which never utter'd or denied a creed !

CCCXII.

THE SONNETEER TO THE SEA-SHELL.

Fair Ocean shell, the poet's art is weak
To utter all thy rich variety !
How thou dost shame him when he tries to speak,
And tell his ear the rapture of his eye !
I cannot paint as very truth requires
The gold-green gleam that o'er thee breaks and roves,
Nor follow up with words thy flying fires,
Where'er the startled rose-light wakes and moves.
Ah ! why perplex with all thy countless hues
The single-hearted sonnet? Fare thee well !
I give thee up to some gay lyric muse,
As fitful as thyself, thy tale to tell :
The quick-spent sonnet cannot do thee right
Nor in one flash deliver all thy light.

CCCXIII.

TO A NIGHTINGALE ON ITS RETURN.

And art thou here again, sweet nightingale,
To reproduce my happy summer mood,
When, as last year, among these shades I stood,
Or from the lattice heard thy thrilling tale ?
This May-tide is but cold ; yet, none the less,
I trust thy tuneful energy to sing
Through the thin leafage of this laggard spring,
With all thy blended joy and plaintiveness.
How often have my lonely steps been led,
By thy sweet voice, on to thy magic tree !
How often has thy wakeful spirit fed
My thoughts with love, and hope, and mystery !
How often hast thou made my weary head
A music chamber for my soul and thee !

CCCXIV.

THE DROWNED SPANIEL.

The day-long bluster of the storm was o'er :
The sands were bright ; the winds had fallen asleep :
And, from the far horizon, o'er the deep
The sunset swam unshadow'd to the shore.
High up the rainbow had not pass'd away,
When roving o'er the shingly beach I found
A little waif, a spaniel newly drown'd ;
The shining waters kiss'd him as he lay.
In some kind heart thy gentle memory dwells,
I said, and, though thy latest aspect tells
Of drowning pains and mortal agony,
Thy master's self might weep and smile to see
His little dog stretch'd on these rosy shells,
Betwixt the rainbow and the golden sea.

CCCXV.

THE CLASSIC CANARY ON ITS DEATH, BY A STUDENT.

A variation on CCXCIX.

Farewell, sweet bird, so winsome and so wise !
How oft I saw thee hop along the page
Of classic poet or historian sage,
With thy low note and quick enquiring eyes.
Methinks,—thou wert so fond of ancient lore,—
A classic welcome in the shades below
Awaits thee, now thy learned life is o'er ;
To fair Elysian meadows thou shalt go,
A pleasant region without rain or storm ;
Perchance, even now, while my fond memory dwells
On all thy quaint, amusing pedantry,
The chirp, the glance, the little saffron form,
From thy small beak old Charon takes a fee,
And leaves thee hopping to the asphodels.

CCCXVI.

GREAT BRITAIN THROUGH THE ICE,

Or, Premature Patriotism.

Methought I lived in the icy times forlorn ;
And, with a fond forecasting love and pride,
I hung o'er frozen England :—'When,' I cried,
' When will the island of our hopes be born ?
When will our fields be seen, our church-bells heard ?
And Avon, Doon, and Tweed break forth in song ?
This blank unstoried ice be warm'd and stirr'd,
And Thames, and Clyde, and Humber roll along
To a free sea-board ? airs of paradise
Instal our summer and our flowery springs,
And lift the larks, and land the nightingales ?
And this wild alien unfamiliar Wales
Melt home among her harps ? and vernal skies
Thaw out old Dover for the houseless kings ? '

CCCXVII.

*TO MRS. CAMERON, FRESHWATER, ISLE
OF WIGHT.*

Lo ! modern beauty lends her lips and eyes
To tell an ancient story.   Thou hast brought
Into thy picture all our fancy sought
Of that old time, with cunning art and wise.
The sun obeys thy gestures, and allows
Thy guiding hand, where'er thou hast a mind,
To turn his passive light upon mankind,
And set his seal and thine on chosen brows.
Thou lovest all loveliness, and many a face
Is press'd and summon'd from the breezy shores
On thine immortal charts to take its place ;
While, near at hand, the jealous ocean roars :
His noblest Tritons would thy subjects be,
And all his fairest Nereids sit to thee.

A A

CCCXVIII.

THE LOVER AND HIS WATCH

As one who eyes his watch, ere day is born,
If haply by its glimmer he may trace
How near he is to some high festal morn,
He sought and found the love-light on her face.
That single glimpse chased all his doubts away,
And left a happy hope, a safe surmise,
A golden guess in darkness : His glad eyes
Had seen enough to prove the coming day.
Thenceforth he felt an ever waxing power
O'er all his weak and timid fears prevail ;
His heart moved forward with the growing hour ;
He felt that gleam of promise would not fail :
That peeping star was trusty, though so dim,
And show'd the morn was near for her and him.

CCCXIX.

BEAU NASH AND THE ROMAN,

Or, the Two Eras.

In that old pump-room, as I stood alone
Beside the Bath, the old waters of the sun,
I thought of two past eras : All were gone
To evening haunts of pleasure and of fun.
As they went off to dine, and dance, and sup,
The Bath began to teem with modish ghosts,
A reach of Lethe, sending bubbles up
From bygone dandies, and forgotten toasts.
Then, for relief, I turn'd to see and hear
An older past, with fancy's eye, that takes
Fond retrospects, and fancy's ear, that makes
A sound of her own longings.   Ofttimes here
A home and grave the peaceful Roman found
And little Caius coo'd on British ground.

CCCXX.

THE LARK'S NEST.

I never hear a lark its matins sing,
But I bethink me of that orphan nest,
Where once I saw a little callow thing,
Erect, with death-cold wings, above the rest,
As tho' he lived and pleaded.   Light and shade
Swept in and out of his poor open maw,
While underneath his silent feet I saw
A short-breathed group of helpless orphans laid.
The life was ebbing from each infant throat,
Too young as yet for music's earliest note ;
High up a living lark sang loud and free—
Keen was the contrast—it was sad to mark
Those eyes, heaven-charter'd, now earth-bound and
　　　dark :
Beneath a morning sky they could not see.

CCCXXI.

OLD STEPHEN.

He served his master well from youth to age ;
Who gave him then a little plot of land,
Enough a busy spirit to engage,
Too small to overtax an aged hand.
Old Stephen's memory hallows all the ground ;
He made this thrifty lawn so spruce and small,
Dial and seat within its narrow bound,
And both half-hid with woodbine from the Hall.
But he is gone at last : how meek he lay
That night, and pray'd his dying hours away—
When the sun rose he ceased to breathe and feel :
Day broke—his eyes were on a lovelier dawn,
While ours beheld the sweet May morning steal
Across his dial and his orphan lawn.

CCCXXII.

THE SIGHING OF THE BOEHMER WALD.

One morn I read the brief memorial lines,
Which told of a great forest's swift decay,
And how they stripp'd the bark from off the pines,
And strove to burn the beetle pest away.
That night the sighing of the Boehmer Wald
Pass'd through my garden in the twilight gloom;
A mighty sigh, the herald of its doom,
For insect hosts move on, but never halt.
Sad was the dirge of those primeval trees,
Grown for a thousand years; nor seem'd it strange
That I, so jealous of the woodman's stroke,
So chary of the lives of pine and oak,
Should catch the sound of sylvan grief and change,
The forest's dying voice across the seas.

CCCXXIII.

PUBLIC AND PRIVATE USE OF THE TELEGRAPH.

O'er the red battlefield, or populous street,
By river shore, or by the railway side,
Or stretch'd on old-world shells beneath the tide,
The wire is laid, our world-wide wants to meet.
The lightning dived, and rose to bring my name
To England, with a message kind and sweet:
And at my beck return'd again, to greet
My distant friend, as swiftly as it came.
'Tis strange to hold in full monopoly,
Even for an instant, that electric spell
Which serves the State, yet plies for thee and me;
And lends itself our homely news to tell:
The mighty moment posts o'er land and sea,
With Willie's birth or Lotty's last farewell.

CCCXXIV.

THE WIDOW'D BRIDEGROOM.

The widow'd Bridegroom sought the winter wood
At eve, for Mary's vows were plighted there:
When, as beneath the wild-rose arch she stood,
He lovingly unwound her golden hair.
The sun had set, the night was cold and still:
There was no stir amongst the leafless trees:
No voices from the hamlet or the hill
Disturb'd his clear and silent memories.
And so he mused and brooded o'er the past:
He lived an hour with Mary's bygone sighs
And smiles ; he re-invoked her dear replies.
But, when he left the hallow'd spot at last,
He kiss'd the night-frost from the dusky spray,
Where bloom'd the wild-rose of their trysting day.

CCCXXV.

THE POSTED SWAN.

A noble swan was borne through field and lane
On to the Squire's, close grappled and convey'd
By walking post ; his haughty neck obey'd
The strenuous grasp : he strain'd his wings in vain.
He could not blush to show his rage and shame :
He had no turkey's trick to pouch his spleen,
And give it colour, though he urged his claim
To freedom with a proud and swan-like mien.
But nilly willy he was haul'd away,
And launch'd upon the lake, his future home ;
Where day by day he sees the postman come,
And linger near him with a fond delay,
While he moves proudly forward to receive
Such dole as royal mails can pause to give.

CCCXXVI.

JULIUS CÆSAR AND THE HONEY-BEE.

Poring on Cæsar's death with earnest eye,
I heard a fretful buzzing in the pane :
' Poor bee ! ' I cried, ' I'll help thee by-and-by ; '
Then dropp'd mine eyes upon the page again.
Alas ! I did not rise ; I help'd him not :
In the great voice of Roman history
I lost the pleading of the window-bee,
And all his woes and troubles were forgot.
In pity for the mighty chief, who bled
Beside his rival's statue, I delay'd
To serve the little insect's present need ;
And so he died for lack of human aid.
I could not change the Roman's destiny ;
I might have set the honey-maker free.

CCCXXVII.

NIGHTINGALES IN LINCOLNSHIRE.

Well I remember how the nightingale,
That linger'd in the genial South so long,
Made his sweet trespass, broke his ancient pale,
And brought into the North his wondrous song.
But, when I thought to hear his first sweet bar,
He sang a mile away : I could not seek
His chosen haunt, for I was faint and weak :
Alas! I cried, so near and yet so far :
Kind nature gather'd all the sounds I love
About my window ; lowings of the kine,
The thrush, the linnet, and the cooing dove ;
But out, alas! how should I not repine,
When, scarce a mile beyond my garden grove,
The night-bird warbled for all ears but mine?

CCCXXVIII.

It was her first sweet child, her heart's delight:
And, though we all foresaw his early doom,
We kept the fearful secret out of sight;
We saw the canker, but she kiss'd the bloom.
And yet it might not be: we could not brook
To vex her happy heart with vague alarms,
To blanch with fear her fond intrepid look,
Or send a thrill through those encircling arms.
She smiled upon him, waking or at rest:
She could not dream her little child would die:
She toss'd him fondly with an upward eye:
She seem'd as buoyant as a summer spray,
That dances with a blossom on its breast,
Nor knows how soon it will be borne away.

CCCXXIX.

ON SHOOTING A SWALLOW IN EARLY YOUTH.

I hoard a little spring of secret tears,
For thee, poor bird ; thy death-blow was my crime :
From the far past it has flow'd on for years ;
It never dries ; it brims at swallow-time.
No kindly voice within me took thy part,
Till I stood o'er thy last faint flutterings ;
Since then, methinks, I have a gentler heart,
And gaze with pity on al wounded wings.
Full oft the vision of thy fallen head,
Twittering in highway dust, appeals to me ;
Thy helpless form, as when I struck thee dead,
Drops out from every swallow-flight I see.
I would not have thine airy spirit laid,
I seem to love the little ghost I made.

CCCXXX.

THE QUIET TIDE NEAR ARDROSSAN.

On to the beach the quiet waters crept:
But, though I stood not far within the land,
No tidal murmur reach'd me from the strand.
The mirror'd clouds beneath old Arran slept.
I look'd again across the watery waste :
The shores were full, the tide was near its height,
Though scarcely heard : the reefs were drowning fast,
And an imperial whisper told the might
Of the outer floods, that press'd into the bay,
Though all besides was silent.   I delight
In the rough billows, and the foam-ball's flight :
  love the shore upon a stormy day ;
But yet more stately were the power and ease
That with a whisper deepen'd all the seas.

CCCXXXI.

AGNES AND ARIES.

Fresh from the page of Virgil's Pollio
I look'd abroad upon the wintry land,
And there I saw two dingy wethers stand
Beside a patch of soil'd and thawing snow.
With Maro's vision burning on mine eyes,
Alas ! I said, how meagre is the view !
No wondrous ram with his spontaneous dyes,
No bright Amomum with its eastern hue !
But winter soon will pass, nor shall we need
Assyrian flowers to deck our May and June ;
No sheep have we of that transcendent stock ;
But Agnes, merriest of our household flock,
Will take a change of shawls into the mead,
And shift at will from saffron to maroon.

CCCXXXII.

ROSE AND CUSHIE.

The cow low'd sadly o'er the distant gate,
In the mid field, and round our garden rail :
But nought her restless sorrow could abate,
Nor patting hands, nor clink of milking pail ;
For she had lost the love she least could spare.
Her little suckling calf, her life of life,
In some far shambles waited for the knife,
And spent his sweet breath on the murderous air.
One single yearning sound, repeated still,
Moan'd from the croft, and wander'd round the hill :
The heedless train ran brawling down the line ;
On went the horseman, and the market cart :
But little Rose, who loved the sheep and kine,
Ran home to tell of Cushie's broken heart.

CCCXXXIII.

TWO SORTS OF EMIGRANTS.

His debts are paid, but all his land is gone ;
He leaves our narrow seas with many a tear,
Bound for the south, dishearten'd and alone,
To use those energies he wasted here.
A colony of larks their passage take
With him.   Small cheer his own sad voyage yields :
The rolling seas contrast his quiet lake,
And fleeting shores his patrimonial fields.
At last he lands, half hopeful, half forlorn,
A human heart with all its cares and ties.
The larks, his fellow emigrants, will rise
At once and sing, on alien breezes borne,
Forget the transfer from their native skies,
And sing as bravely to the southern morn.

CCCXXXIV.

TO A GERMAN LADY.

We took thee with our English youths and maids
ı
To spend a day among the forest shades,
From noise and city tumult far away.
We heard thee singing in thy native tongue,
Of the rich beauties of thy Rhineland vale,
While still the sunset beam and morning gale
Were sweet recurring words in thy wild song.
We gather'd round thy seat, a listening band;
And one fond youth soon proffer'd heart and hand,
And wedded thee beside thy native Rhine,
And chose his home in thy dear fatherland,
Where now he hears at will that voice of thine
Sing *Morgenluft* and *Abendsonnenschein.*

¹ A line has been omitted here from the manuscript. The
sonnet is not in the author's hand-writing.

CCCXXXV.

TO A GREEK GIRL ON THE SEA SHORE.

There are no heathen gods to play the rogue
With wandering maidens, as in olden time ;
Whose wild Olympian hearts were all agog
To choose their victim, and inflict their crime :
Thou hast been gathering flowers, a fragrant store,
But no grim Dis has seiz'd thee for his bride ;
And though thou rovest on this houseless shore
No horned Zeus betrays thee to the tide.
Olympus is gone by ; but thou art there,
The ward of truer heavens, all pure and sweet :
No lust nor guile thy lonely path shall meet :
The Father's Self, Who made thee good and fair,
And pours His gentle waves about thy feet,
Upholds thy virgin footsteps everywhere.

CCCXXXVI.

THE WEDDING POSY.

Thanks to thy newly-wedded hand, which gave
These bridal honours to the tomb to-day,
A daughter's wedding posy ! Who shall say
It is a truant at a father's grave?
O'er the blue hills, fair Edith, thou art gone ;
Thou and thy votive flowers are sunder'd wide ;
But still ye are so tenderly allied
On earth, that your twin sweetness shall be one
In heaven.   Our Father's eye shall ne'er reprove
The bride's recurrence to the daughter's love.
And when thou hast fulfill'd thy days and hours,
And thy pure life its meed of glory brings,
The earliest passage of thine angel wings
Among the blest shall tell of orange flowers !

CCCXXXVII.

MILLIE MACGILL.

I watch'd thy merry gambols on the sand,
And ask'd thy name beside the morning sea ;
Sweet came thine answer, with thy little hand
Upon the spade, and thy blue eyes on me,
Millie Macgill. I know not where thou art,
Since that brief greeting by Ardrossan shore,
But still thy guileless voice delights my heart,
Though I should never see nor hear thee more.
Where art thou, little darling of the past ?
Since that bright morn the silent years have flown,
And now thy beauty must be fully grown :
Dost thou still live? Art thou unwedded still?
Or are those silver sounds disjoined at last,
Thy seaside names of Millie and Macgill?

CCCXXXVIII.

TO BEATRICE ON HER FIRST INTERVIEW
WITH DANTE.

Daughter of Portinari, thou hast met
This eve the bard of Hell and Paradise :
By love's own hand the very hour was set
For thy glad greeting, and his sweet surprise.
In that short interview his loving eye
Hath seized thy fair belongings, and distrain'd
Thy crimson gown to dress his dreams with joy,
And flame across his lonely hours.   He gain'd
A prize in meeting thee, and thou hast part
Henceforth in him, to all his fame allied :
For thou hast pass'd into a poet's heart,
To be his Beatrice, his angel-guide.
Hail ! little handmaid of a great renown,
With thine eight summers and thy crimson gown !

CCCXXXIX.

CALVUS TO A FLY.

Ah! little fly, alighting fitfully
In the dim dawn on this bare head of mine,
Which spreads a white and gleaming track for thee,
When chairs and dusky wardrobes cease to shine.
Though thou art irksome, let me not complain;
Thy foolish passion for my hairless head
Will spend itself, when these dark hours are sped,
And thou shalt seek the sunlight on the pane.
But still beware! thou art on dangerous ground:
An angry sonnet, or a hasty hand,
May slander thee, or crush thee: thy shrill sound
And constant touch may shake my self-command:
And thou mayst perish in that moment's spite,
And die a martyr to thy love of light.

CCCXL.

COWPER'S THREE HARES.

They know not of their mission from above,
These little hares, that through the coppice stray;
Nor how they will take rank, some future day,
As friends of sorrow, and allies of love.
To their wild haunts a friendly thief shall come,
And take them hence, no more to rove at will,
Till those three gentle hearts grow gentler still,
And ready for the mourning poet's home.
Hail, little triad, peeping from the fern,
Ye have a place to fill, a name to earn!
Far from the copse your tender mission lies,—
To soothe a soul, too sad for trust and prayer,
To gambol round a woe ye cannot share,
And mix your woodland breath with Cowper's sighs.

CCCXLI.

A COUNTRY DANCE.

He has not woo'd, but he has lost his heart.
That country dance is a sore test for him ;
He thinks her cold ; his hopes are faint and dim ;
But though with seeming mirth she takes her part
In all the dances and the laughter there,
And though to many a youth, on brief demand,
She gives a kind assent and courteous hand,
She loves but him, for him is all her care.
With jealous heed her lessening voice he hears
Down that long vista, where she seems to move
Among fond faces and relays of love,
And sweet occasion, full of tender fears :
Down those long lines he watches from above,
Till with the refluent dance she reappears.

CCCXLII.

SHADOWS OFF THE COAST.

The moon was bright, and o'er the tranquil flood
She sped the silver ripples to the shore,
Where in yon sea-side house two lovers stood,
Once more to part, and then to part no more.
The table lamp with its reflected ray
Brought out two human figures on the bay,
Through the closed window, phantom-like and thin
But timing all the gestures from within.
Oh! with what loving laughter did they gaze
On their own forms, and on that mimic blaze!
But, when she left the spot, his eyes grew dim:
She pass'd at once by sea and land from him:
She was no longer at his side, and he
Sat by his lonely lamp on land and sea.

LYRICS.

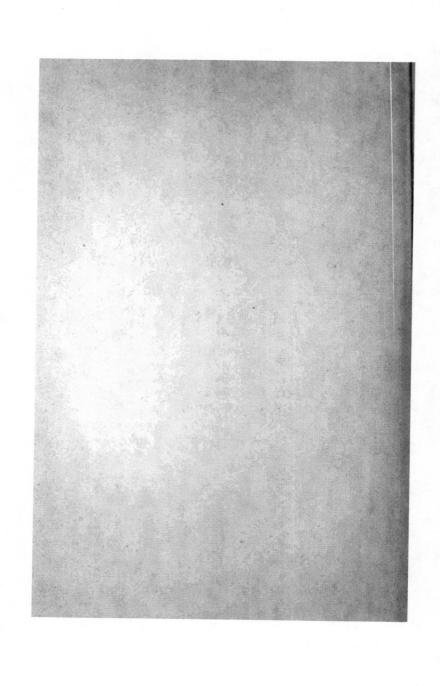

I.

THE ALTAR.

How fondly look'd I on the place,
   Assign'd to rites of spousal love !
How holy seem'd that Board of Grace,
   With Jesus blessing bread above !

'Twas bosom'd in a kindlier air,
   Than the outer realms of care and dole ;
A sense of Godhead brooded there,
   Whose spell-like silence lull'd the soul.

And, though full oft the accents dear
   Here utter'd, had been falsely fond ;
Still they were breathed and plighted here,
   And broken in a place beyond !

II.

*A LEGEND FROM DE LAMARTINE'S TRAVELS IN
THE EAST, VERSIFIED.*

It was upon a Lammas night
Two brothers woke and said,
As each upon the other's weal
Bethought him on his bed ;

The elder spake unto his wife,
Our brother dwells alone ;
No little babes to cheer his life,
And helpmate hath he none.

Up will I get and of my heap
A sheaf bestow or twain,
The while our Ahmed lies asleep,
And wots not of the gain.

So up he got and did address
Himself with loving heed,
Before the dawning of the day,
To do that gracious deed.

Now to the younger, all unsought,
The same kind fancy came !
Nor wist they of each other's thought,
Though movèd to the same.

Abdallah, he hath wife, quoth he,
And little babes also ;
What would be slender boot to me,
Would make his heart o'erflow.

Up will I get, and of my heap
A sheaf bestow or twain,
The while he sweetly lies asleep,
And wots not of the gain.

So up he got and did address
Himself with loving heed,
Before the dawning of the day,
To mate his brother's deed !

Thus play'd they oft their gracious parts,
And marvell'd oft to view
Their sheaves still equal, for their hearts
In love were equal too.

One morn they met, and wondering stood,
To see by clear daylight,
How each upon the other's good
Bethought him in the night.

So when this tale to him was brought,
The Caliph did decree,
Where twain had thought the same good thought
There Allah's House should be.

III.

AN INCIDENT ON THE DEE.

A mournful tale was told to me :
Poor Jehu, new to sail and oar,
Upon the rapid river's tide
Embark'd his little children four ;
But swamp'd the skiff he could not guide,
And drown'd them all in Dee.

And often, when with calm command
He reins his master's steeds so free,
While four sweet children sit behind,
To his long-trusted care consign'd,
He feels, ' It is the self-same hand
That drown'd mine own in Dee.'

IV.[1]

The council of the brave are met,
Soon will their swords with blood be wet,
The blood of tyranny and pride,
On—on—this is not regicide !

He thinks his sand is not outrun,
But he shall start to find it done ;
He mocketh at our bold emprize,
Though freedom looks him in the eyes.

What claim have they on further breath
For momentary league with death,
Who dare to make the human heart
Throb with the fears themselves impart ?

And he hath done this shameless deed,
Thus answer'd in a nation's need ;
He link'd our fetters to his crown
So tight, they burst, and flung him down.

---

[1] Published in 1827.

When kings demand with haughtiest aims
Beyond their weight of kingly claims,
With worthy scorn and anger stirr'd,
We fill the balance with the sword !

Slaves, each and all, our necks have borne
His yoke with grief that swallow'd scorn
Till, galling deeper, it began
To make all men, and each a man !

We seek a soil for hope to thrive—
But where is hope, if tyrants live ?
We burn to draw a bolder breath,
By quenching his in forceful death !

V.

Ye mighty forests, deep and old,
   With knotty stems and towering shade,
That where the lordly streams are roll'd
   A dense and matted gloom have made,

Your arms are rife with germs of life,
   Your heads receive the rushing wind;
With lingering sweeps the night-breeze creeps
   O'er your thick robes and wrinkled rind;

Ye stand like shrouds before the clouds
   That hold the sunset of mid-June—
And darker still when o'er the hill
   Creeps the pale dawning of the moon.

O then the soft suffusion clear
   Peers over your enormous screen,
The skies are white with silver light,
   How grand the shade! how sweet the sheen!

And when the sun's first rosy line
   Is drawn i' the east—thro' every glade
Aglow with golden dews ye shine
   And orange-tints your depths pervade!

VI.

A FATHER TO HIS SLEEPING CHILD.[1]

Thy lips, my child, recall the smile
  Of those I would not show thee now,
And she who blest my life awhile
  Hath left her spirit on thy brow :
O doubly dear, now she is cold,
I would not hear thy death-bell toll'd !

Her voice was musical and low,
  Of thrilling tone like sounds in sleep ;
And, like the footfall in the snow,
  Heard faintly, though it sank so deep :
And thy soft accents are the same,
Thou hast her voice—her look—her name !

---

[1] The last stanza of this and the fourth stanza of the next
poem were marked by Coleridge for approval.

MY MOTHER.

Think'st thou if spirits pure as thine
    Through life might be for ever near,
I should not every fear resign,
    As from my boyhood's home I steer?

A mother heard our infant cries,
    And folded us with fond embrace,
And when we woke, our infant eyes
    Were opened on a mother's face.

Our wishes she did make her own,
    Her bosom fed and pillow'd too,
Answering each start or fitful moan
    With trembling pulses fond and true.

Then knowledge was a thing untaught;
    Heaven's charity, a daily dole,
Stole in inaudibly, and wrought
    Its gentle bonds about the soul.

And oh! if spirits pure as thine
    Through life might be for ever near,
There would be scantier chance that mine
    Would sink beneath the doom I fear!

Spottiswoode & Co., Printers, New-street Square, London.

Printed in the United States
116417LV00005B/107/A

9 780548 722572